On the Potomac River

From the Fairfax Stone to Smith Point Lighthouse

Douglas Campbell & Thomas Sherman

Dedication

This book is dedicated to our patient wives,
Trish Campbell and Marilyn Sherman, who lost us during more
than three years of weekend jaunts up and down the Potomac River.

Acknowledgments

During the more than three years it took to travel the length of the Potomac and to write and paint about the river, we had the good fortune to meet many gracious people along the way who gave us their time, advice, and support. Many of those who helped us never knew we were writing and painting a book about the Potomac River. They were just the kind of people that were not afraid to help strangers. Their friendliness toward strangers must have something to do with making your living on or near the water. Although somewhat wary of strangers ourselves, we couldn't imagine leaving a stranger drifting in a boat without stopping to offer assistance. This attitude is prevalent among most sailors. It's an unwritten rule among sailors that a distress call is answered by all who can offer aid. Even those who speed by on motorboats and curse slower-moving sailboats have come to the rescue of engineless sailboats when the winds have died. So, for all those nameless people who gave us directions, who grabbed our lines and helped us tie up to the docks we visited, who answered our questions and made us feel like we were doing the right thing, we thank you. We can also put names to the faces of many others that have helped us:

As a long-time friend, Stephen J. Chant provided countless hours of editing and lent words of encouragement to us during periods of writer's or artist's block! Joseph Burnside and Art Schwartz for their aviation piloting skills; Ann Devers, a friend from our earlier days with the Aviation and Space Writers Association, for her words of encouragement and for locating the Waterfront Museum in Old Town, Alexandria; and John Fisher, who spent many hours running his Chris-Craft motorboat up and down the river for us. The late Mike Freeman, owner of American Watersports in Oxon Hill, Maryland, for his incredible stories about the Potomac and for the use of his inflatable boat. A thanks to the good people at the U.S. National Park Service; Library of Congress; Fairfax County, Virginia, and Prince Georges County, Maryland, Public Library systems for assisting us in our research. Lastly, a heartfelt thanks to Cheryl Gavid for her formatting genius in balancing text with the images.

Foreword

Tom and I planned on depicting scenes of life along the shore as seen from the perspective of actually being on the Potomac River. We wanted to see the land that the Potomac passes in its 383-mile journey from a logical perspective - that of being on the Potomac waters looking at points of interest along both shorelines. We saw the natural settings of the forests, rocks and falls (Great Falls, Little Falls, Three Sisters Rocks, Mather Gorge), the convergence of other rivers into the Potomac (the Shenandoah River at Harpers Ferry, the Eastern Branch of the Potomac at Washington, D.C., now called Anacostia River) and the architecture of man-made points of interest (Mount Vernon, the John F. Kennedy Center for the Performing Arts, Harper's Ferry, Fort Washington).

This was done in a variety of ways over a period of three years at all times of day (and sometimes night), in all seasons, and in all types of weather. We actually waded into the shallow streams at the headwaters of the Potomac, and floated down most of the river in an inflatable boat, a Chris-Craft powerboat, and the SPIRIT OF WASHINGTON (a cruise ship homeported in Washington, D.C.). We stood on the frozen Potomac in winter, and even floated on and dived under the river dressed in wetsuits and SCUBA gear. We came to understand the important role that the Potomac played in our Nation's history - from its creation, to its "discovery" by Captain John Smith, through the Civil War and great floods, to its struggle back from man-made pollution, to its proud appearance today. We also came to learn bits of geology, ornithology, zoology, botany, and many other sciences to help us understand the Potomac.

The winding Potomac took us through four distinct geographical areas. The first area encountered was the Appalachian highlands of the westernmost portion of Maryland and the northern portion of West Virginia, which took us northeast past Massanutten Mountain. Here we crossed into the second geographical area—Maryland's Cumberland Valley (called Shenandoah Valley in Virginia) where we found ourselves passing through the Blue Ridge Mountains and other minor valleys east of the Blue Ridge. Just downstream of Harpers Ferry at Point of Rocks, Maryland, we would follow the Potomac as it penetrated the last mountain barrier, the Catoctins, and emerge into the third geographical area—the rolling Piedmont country. By all the laws of Nature, the Potomac could only flow downhill and downstream, and it could have backed up and become a huge lake, using the Blue Ridge as an immense natural dam. Instead, as the mountains were pushed slowly upwards millions of years ago, the Potomac simply began carving away into the soft bedrock and earth and entrenched itself into a path through the mountains from which it would never stray. Overflowing sometimes, it always returned to its original riverbed. Lastly, just above Washington, D.C., we watched as the Potomac ran furiously over Great and Little Falls and into the fourth and final geographical area—the brackish Tidewater area where the waters become affected by the tidal pulls of the sun and moon.

Our transit down the Potomac through these four distinct landscapes gave Tom and I the variety we needed for this project. We gained an indescribable amount of information from our travels on the Potomac. At almost every bend we encountered something different, from mountain laurel to hydrilla, from birds found only in the higher elevations to blue herons and other tidal shorebirds. We drifted in slow moving waters through the Piedmont plains and observed roaring falls from the safety of shore. At every turn of the river a new personality became evident - the incredible and innumerable smells, sights and sounds of the river.

When we began this book, we thought that we could do research in a library and just float down the river. Then, we reasoned, the readers would only have to understand what the writer and artist, using their respective media, were trying to tell them about the river. What happened, though, was that the Potomac became a teacher and we the students. As the months progressed, the book took on a new meaning; it was no longer important that we impress upon our readers with how much we knew about the river. It became important that the reader come to understand the river more than to understand the writer and the artist. In that we hope we succeeded.

Table of Contents

CHAPTER 1

From the Fairfax Stone, West Virginia to Paw Paw, West Virginia

The downstream journey begins.

Just as there are several sources of water that could be considered the beginning of the Potomac River, there are just as many written sources laying claim to the river's beginning. One written source claims that the river "has its beginnings in the western part of Virginia, where the South Branch is a small rill west of Monterey near Hightown." In reality, the Potomac begins where one chooses to believe it begins.

Tom and I agreed that, for our purposes, the Potomac's life begins where it comes out of the Allegheny Mountains on the Backbone Mountain range. The Potomac begins more than 3,300 feet above sea level and near the highest point in Maryland. This is the North Branch of the Potomac. The exact spot we have agreed to is in West Virginia, a few hundred feet from the state border with Maryland. The exact spot is at a point called the Fairfax Stone, a West Virginia State Historical Monument. Having convinced myself, and then Tom, that no book about a river could be complete without visiting its source, the Fairfax Stone became our starting point. In anticipation, we packed the Volkswagen Vanagon the night before our departure. Our interest in finding this spot was not original. The source of the Potomac has captured people's imagination almost from the time the Potomac was "discovered" by Captain John Smith in 1608. On June 16, 1608, Captain Smith sailed into the Potomac River from the Chesapeake Bay. His printed narrative states: "A River ... fed by many sweet Rivers and Springs which fall from the bordering Hills ... the River exceedeth with abundance of fish ... there runneth many fayre brookes of Christel-like water ... and abundance of fish, lying so thick with their heads above the water, as for the want of nets." He then ran aground, at which time he disembarked and thrust his sword into the water, spearing a fish.

The name Potomac has had several translations and spellings, but the original word "Potomek" came from Captain Smith when he discovered an Indian "King's House" along the river that the Algonquin Indians called "Potomek." From that the river itself got its name. In Algonquin language, Potomac means "where something is brought" or "trading place." The ancient Greek word for river is "potamos," but how the presence of such a word from an Old World language became a word in the American Indian language before the "rediscovery" of these Indians can only be guessed. Since 1608, however, Potomac has been spelled Potomek, Potomack, Potowmack, Patowmack, and at least six other variations. For the early settlers, how it was spelled or its origin was of little importance compared to the need to make a living from it and to survive in the wilderness.

We would not be riding horses and pulling wagons like the earlier settlers, but driving and hiking up the remote Appalachian hillside to capture the emergence of the river on film, paper and canvas. Our horsepower was in the rear of the camper that Tom and I packed with the essentials of survival: tent, sleeping bags, food and water. We would begin our longest trek early the next morning.

Tom and I were awake and on the road before the sun rose. The cloudy sky prevented us from seeing the sunrise, but it soon began getting light. We stopped at a convenience store for coffee and then it was time to accelerate forward on our first official Potomac trip.

Being more of a "morning person" than Tom, I was driving and noticed Tom drifting back to sleep, so I began talking to him.

"You know, Tom, ever since we were roommates back in college, we've done some pretty interesting things. I'm really looking forward to getting a book published about the Potomac."

Tom rolled his eyes, knowing it would be hard to get any sleep with me talking. Tom and I know each other pretty well by now. We were roommates back at the University of Kansas many years ago and had gone through college as midshipmen in the Navy Reserve Officers' Training Corps (NROTC) together after awarded full scholarships. We received our Bachelors' degrees and were commissioned as officers in the U.S. Navy the same day. We attended Surface Warfare Officers' School in Newport, Rhode Island, and later we joined the Navy Reserves. I was Tom's best man at his wedding. We are diving buddies from the first year we learned to SCUBA and probably know what each one is thinking before the other one says anything. We've crewed together on sailboats from Rhode Island to the Caribbean to the Florida Keys. All told, we've become pretty good friends over the years. Now we can add another thing to that list. This was going to be our first book together, with Tom providing the watercolor paintings and I providing the words.

As we continued west on Interstate 70, we talked about how we considered ourselves relative newcomers to the Potomac River, having both recently settled in this region of the United States. In retrospect, we were both a bit naive to the depth and breadth of the river. Not only about the physical size of the river, because that was apparent on the charts we had of the river. It was the sheer capacity of one river to hold so many stories that captivated us. It was the stories about the part the Potomac played in the development and history of the United States: its floods, its role in the Civil War, the use of its water for the Chesapeake & Ohio Canal, the quotes about the Potomac from men like George Washington and Thomas Jefferson, its near-death by pollution and its subsequent return to life, and even its role in the invention of steam-powered boats. Tom and I were not the first ones to venture out onto the river; yet there were things waiting to be rediscovered as we started out on our own journey. What lay ahead would keep us looking forward to the next bend in the river in the expectation of finding something else to capture our senses.

We continued westward, but the coffee was catching up with us and the Interstate rest stop just west of Frederick was a welcome relief. Here, on our way to the Fairfax Stone, was the first surprise of the trip. At the rest stop we came across an interesting sign. I have heard President Dwight D. Eisenhower called many things, but never the "Father of the Interstate Highway System." The sign read that in August 1973, the U.S. Congress designated a cross-country stretch of interstate as the "Dwight D. Eisenhower Highway." This was done in tribute to President Eisenhower's early recognition of the need for a national network of highways.

Eisenhower saw the need to enhance the mobility of a growing nation. His dream originated in 1919 on an Army convoy from Washington, D.C., to San Francisco, California, a journey that took 62 days. On June 29, 1956, President Eisenhower signed the historic legislation that created the National System of Interstate and Defense Highways and the Federal Highway Trust Fund. These were pay-as-you-go mechanisms through which motorists have funded the construction and upkeep of the U.S. highway system. Today, that system stands as a monument to Eisenhower's vision as a young Army officer—a legacy of safety and mobility that has brought all Americans closer together.

Westward we continued, motoring along on Interstate 70 until we reached Hancock, Maryland. Driving around Hancock, we watched the Potomac glide past the town on its downstream run toward the Chesapeake Bay. Crossing the river by bridge into West Virginia, we followed a road that ran parallel with the river. We were interested in seeing if there were any apparent dangers to us in our upcoming downstream boat trip through the area. Noting none, we logged this piece of information in our brains for later use. Backtracking, we crossed the same bridge again and continued our westward journey. We found ourselves travelling on Route 40 into Cumberland where the Chesapeake and Ohio Canal (better known as the C&O Canal) ends. Here we stopped at the Cumberland Train Station to stretch our legs. The station is now a museum to the trains and the canal. As we walked along the railroad tracks, we looked back at Wills Creek pouring into the Potomac. The North Branch of the Potomac and Wills Creek were both running high due to recent rains. We walked down to the soggy shoreline to get an idea on how we would navigate through this area of the Potomac, just as we did at Hancock. It was there that we saw the waterfall, a drop of some 8 feet of churning muddy Potomac water dropping out from under a bridge. Tom and I just looked at each other.

"No way are we going to run our boat through all the North Branch of the Potomac," I said, pointing to the waterfall.

"This isn't on any of our maps," Tom replied.

As prepared as we were for the journey, we still wondered what other surprises the Potomac would have in store for us. While watching the water drop over the man-made falls and wondering about what other surprises were to come our way, I suddenly remembered something.

"Hey, Tom," I said. "I remember reading something about whitewater canoeists rating the North Branch of the Potomac near Kitzmiller as one of the most challenging stretches of rapids on the East Coast." Taking a leisurely trip down the river had suddenly become an impossible mission.

It was then that I silently decided I would be taking photographs of Tom in that foaming water from the safety of the shore. Tom and I agree to a basic philosophy: that life must be risked occasionally to make living worthwhile. I knew that staying in our inflatable boat as we drifted downstream into the Kitzmiller area would give a clear measure of the worth we put on our respective lives.

The wind picked up and felt like it was blowing right through my coat. A snow squall was moving toward us, so we aborted our short hike and returned to the camper.

It was April 1, and as if to commemorate April Fools' Day, the snow squall had hit us. When we found the Fairfax Stone, there would be an inch of snow on the ground. Peering through the streaks left by the windshield wipers, we were moving closer to our destination.

The roadmaps of Maryland, Virginia and West Virginia went back to the glove compartment. Out came the U.S. Department of the Interior Geological Survey 7.5-minute topographic map of the Davis Quadrangle. We had prepared to find this one stone among all the stones surrounding us, yet even the charts didn't give us enough information on exactly how to get to the Fairfax Stone. If there had been any signs directing us, they would have been covered with wet snow. We chose to turn and follow the Western Maryland railroad tracks and then hike about a mile up the hill on which the Fairfax Stone was placed.

At the top of the hill we stopped and looked around. We found nothing that suggested we were even on the right hill.

"I'm going to climb that pile of slate," Tom said. "You walk around to the left and see what you can find."

Strip mining pushed up the slate and when Tom finally got to the summit he took some fantastic camera shots. Atop this artificial hilltop he scanned the horizon in a complete circle and noted that all the other hilltops were below him. He was literally on top of the world in this part of the world.

With Tom heading in one direction, I walked around to the left of the slate heap until I came across a sign with an arrow on it. I brushed the snow off the sign and read "Fairfax Stone," but the sign was lying flat on the ground. We were close, but the arrow on the sign could have been pointing in any direction. Tom climbed down from the slate heap to join me and we headed toward a wooden fence.

"All right, Doug," Tom said, "you've been too quiet. You're either afraid we're lost or you're out of breath from climbing up the hill. How about telling me something about this rock?"

"I'm going to have to rely on some material I found at the Fairfax County library," I answered, pulling out my notes. "'The original Charter of 1632 from King Charles I defined the Maryland state boundaries. It was stated that 'Potowmack's first fountain' was the southernmost point of the state's most western border.'"

That was all right until one had to choose from the many springs that could be entitled to that honor. There is Laurel Run, Buffalo Creek, Sand Run, and many unnamed sources closer to the spring finally chosen. I continued reading: "It was Colonel William Mayo that led the first expedition in 1736 to trace the North Branch of the Potomac. Ten years later a second party placed the Fairfax Stone at the beginning of this same spring."

"Well, Tom," I said, doing some quick calculating in my head, "Two hundred and forty two years later, we're reenacting the same scene."

Walking down a slight incline, we arrived at a parking lot. We saw warning signs about trespassing nailed into trees and a trash can whose lid was chained to the can. We had reached civilization, which meant that the Fairfax Stone was near. Seconds later we found it.

We were obviously the first people there that day as no footprints were seen pressed into the freshly fallen snow. Although the original stone had long since met its fate at the hands of vandals, the replica of the original Fairfax Stone that we inspected was still impressive. After spending hours driving and then walking up this hill, it was like finding the Holy Grail. The wind whipped around us on top of this world; the snow blew into our faces and stuck to our camera lenses. We left the site with only our footprints in the snow to show that we had been there. We had taken pictures from various angles and marveled at the Potomac as it appeared from beneath the rocks next to another stone marker. This stone had a plaque set in it that stated that this monument at the headsprings of the Potomac River marks one of the historic spots of America.

The name "Fairfax Stone" is derived from Thomas Lord Fairfax who owned all the land lying between the Potomac and Rappahannock Rivers. The first Fairfax Stone was marked with an "FX" and was set in

The Fairfax Stone — A Closeup

place in 1746 by Thomas Lewis, a surveyor employed by Lord Fairfax. The Fairfax Stone is now the base point for the western dividing line between Maryland and West Virginia.

The water flowing out from under the rocks was cold to the touch. Red and yellow autumn leaves preserved under the cold clear water retained their brilliant colors, even in April.

"Well Tom," I said, having exhausted a roll of film, "Now it's time to start what we set out to do; travel the length of the Potomac."

"Yep. Point Lookout here we come."

We followed the stream west and then north as it curved its way down the mountain. Near the wooden fence that surrounds the historic site, we stood in the middle of the Potomac River. Only the soles of our boots got wet. When the stream was halfway down the mountain it was more than ankle deep and small tributaries could be seen dribbling into the deepening waters. Further down the mountain the Potomac slipped through a large pipe that ran under a dirt road. We could have walked erect through the pipe but the water was too deep. Tom and I, standing in the culvert, agreed that the road now above our heads was going over the Potomac's first bridge. There was enough water now that it made a gurgling sound as it flowed out from under the pipe and down a small embankment of rocks.

Further downstream we encountered the Potomac's second bridge, a solid wooden bridge no more than 8 feet across. This bridge was built to allow cars to cross the stream at the bottom of North Branch Valley and into Kempton, Maryland. Just past the bridge we were greeted with a small hand painted sign stating simply: "Welcome to Maryland."

"Hey Doug," Tom said, "What's this place?"

"Kempton," I replied, already turning pages in my notebook. Kempton is the closest town to Fairfax Stone and was established by the Davis Coal and Coke Company in 1913. The company mined the local veins of coal, some of the richest in the Upper Potomac Valley. Kempton began as a model town, a showpiece for the company, and we saw cookie-cutter houses all in a row along what could only be considered the main street. The town once had a company store, a grade school, high school and the Kempton Boy's Band.

If one word could categorize Marylanders living in this part of the state, one small hand painted sign summed it up: proud. Kempton was a mining town that had already seen its heyday. Some residents could have moved on to more prosperous towns or cities. Many did, but some decided to stay.

It was late afternoon when we walked through Kempton. Two elderly gentlemen in faded denim overalls and heavy black boots were the only inhabitants we saw. Out by the main road, one leaned against a fencepost while the other had his hands resting in his back pockets. The snow had stopped and blue sky was taking over the heavens as the clouds were pushed away. Their topic of conversation was probably us. We waved from a distance and they returned our wave, but neither group approached the other. They kept talking to each other, but their heads continued to swivel around, their eyes hard on us, as we walked by.

We continued following the Potomac, the water now three to six feet wide and deep enough to drop in a boat or fishing line. We were still in the shadow of the same mountain that spawned the river. High above our heads and to our right was the Fairfax Stone; to our left were Kempton and the remains of the once-prosperous mining company. Just downstream past

Kempton we found where the Potomac widened and broke into several smaller rivulets. It had become shallow enough for us to hop across the smaller streams and back into West Virginia, where we climbed back to the camper.

The high altitude clouds continued to spit snow. We spent the night in front of a roaring fire in the fireplace of a rented cabin at the Blackwater Falls State Park. The tent and camping gear remained securely stowed in the camper.

The North Branch of the Potomac plays an important geographical and political role. The Potomac marks the state boundaries between Maryland and West Virginia at Kempton, and remains the state boundary all the way to Harpers Ferry. From Harpers Ferry, the Potomac then marks the state boundaries of Maryland and Virginia to a point just upstream of Chain Bridge in Washington, D.C. The Potomac then marks the boundaries between the District of Columbia and Virginia from just upstream of the Chain Bridge to the Woodrow Wilson Memorial Bridge; and back to the state boundaries between Virginia and Maryland from the Woodrow Wilson Bridge to where the Potomac flows into the Chesapeake at Point Lookout, Maryland, and Smith Point, Virginia. The Potomac River belongs to the state of Maryland by virtue of a treaty between Maryland and Virginia covering the river and the Chesapeake Bay, a treaty discussed in detail later in this book.

We followed the Potomac from its descent off Backbone Mountain all the way to the Chesapeake Bay. For now, though, our journey was just beginning as we headed off in a predominantly northeast direction through the valley-and-ridge country of the Appalachian highlands toward Cumberland. Before reaching Cumberland, we passed through the towns of Kempton, Bayard, and, at an altitude of 2,312 feet, the town of Gormania, West Virginia, and Gorman, Maryland. One would think that there should be some connection between these two towns besides a bridge across the Potomac and a state boundary. With a little research, we discovered that the railroad companies had something to say about naming towns.

It was around 1881 when the expanding West Virginia Central and Pittsburgh Railroad's train tracks finally reached the town of Schaeffersville. It was the railroad company that got Schaeffersville changed to Elkins. The name was in honor of Senator Stephen B. Elkins from West Virginia who just happened to be a major stockholder of the railroad. The railroad didn't consider that another town in West Virginia already was called Elkins. The people from the original town of Elkins started to complain, so the railroad had to change the name of the town again. This time they changed it to Gormania, in honor of Senator A.P. Gorman, a business associate of Senator Elkins. All this was interesting, because Gormania is in West Virginia and the train station and tracks are located across the Potomac in Maryland. So it appears that the railroad company, indifferent to state boundaries, created the illusion that there was a town around a solitary train station in Maryland. They named that town Gorman. Eventually homes did spring up in Gorman; today both towns are practically deserted.

Continuing, we passed Schell and Harrison, past Maryland's Potomac State Forest, past the water runoff from Mt. Storm Lake in West Virginia, and past the towns of Kitzmiller, Blaine and Chafee. Kitzmiller was named for the pioneer family of Kitzmiller after formerly being called Blaine. It was the chief mining center of the area and in the early 1900s boasted a population of 1,500. Nearby another town was formed, presumably by those who left Kitzmiller, because they called this new town Blaine. The river continues to flow past these towns and then fills the dammed Bloomington Lake before running past the towns of Barnum, Windom, Bloomington and Luke, Maryland. Luke was named for the Luke family who started the paper mill here in 1888. The mill was America's first commercially successful sulfite pulp mill and today it is one of the world's largest paper mills. It can be seen, and smelled, for miles, in spite of the expensive pollution control devices installed. The mill operates 24 hours a day, 7 days a week turning out 1,000 tons of high quality paper a day.

When we reached Westernport, Maryland, we found that water from the Savage River and the Westernport Reservoir flows into the North Branch of the Potomac. Westernport owes its name to the fact that it was the westernmost point that coal was loaded and shipped down the Potomac in the days when Georges Creek Valley was a giant coal-producing area. It was also a point of debarkation for westward journeys across America. Before its more dignified name, Westernport was called Hard Scrabble.

Savage River was the site of the first World Kayaking Championship held in the summer of 1989. Across the river at Westernport is Piedmont, West Virginia. The name Piedmont means "at the foot of the mountain" and here it is the foot of the Alleghenies.

From the whitewater rapids, the river turned 90 degrees to the right and began flowing out of the valley in a southeast direction. We passed the bridge connecting McCoole, Maryland, and Keyser, West Virginia; the bridge we had earlier crossed over in our trip toward the Fairfax Stone. Even small towns like Keyser can hold their place in the history books.

The town of Keyser was named for William Keyser, an official of the Baltimore & Ohio railroad. Keyser changed hands 14 times during the Civil War. Other towns along the Potomac played large roles in the Civil War. West Virginia wasn't even a state until the Civil War when they seceded from Virginia in a dispute over taxes to pay for the war. A reminder of the days when West Virginia was a part of Virginia still exists: both states share the cardinal as the same state bird.

The river turned abruptly 90 degrees again, this time to the left, and returned to flowing in a northeast direction. The river passed the Maryland towns at the base of Dans Mountain along Route 220, including Dawson, Danville, Rawlings, Pinto, Cresaptown, and the suburban towns of Potomac Park, Bowling Green, and Ridgely. Dawson was presumably named after the town's postmaster, Thomas W. Dawson, who was the first Dawson appearing in an 1883 register. One could make a guess that the nearby town of Danville was named after the fact that it lies in the shadow of Dans Mountain. However, it is not named for the mountain but rather for Brother Dan McNally, a minister who died in a plane accident. Rawlings was named for Colonel Moses Rawlings who commanded a Maryland rifle regiment in 1776 and was later in charge of Fort Frederick. The town of Pinto, Maryland, is really called Potomac, with the town of Pinto actually being in West Virginia. However, the Pinto Post Office is in Potomac, so the maps and charts all show Pinto as being in Maryland. The name is supposed to have been taken from the fact that a rider who delivered mail to the Mail Drop rode a pinto horse for many years. We were moving closer to Cumberland.

Cresaptown was named for Joseph Cresap, son of Daniel Cresap, who built a road that led people, including George Washington, through Georges Creek Basin. It was along this road where Cresap had uncovered a phenomenally rich 14-foot wide vein of coal. Besides being an official of the Ohio Company and feuding with the Pennsylvanians, Cresap was noted for floating down the Potomac River in a stout boat. He would carry his gentleman's costume in a waterproof wrapping for when he reached the more provincial towns along the water's edge such as Cumberland, Hancock, Williamsport, Harpers Ferry and Washington. He shortly gave up the trips when he felt that the river had become too crowded, which usually occurred at Cumberland. A monument in Riverside Park in Cumberland commemorates the Cresaps. Joseph Cresap's house, extensively

remodeled, still stands at 198 Oakwood Avenue. Still closer to Cumberland is Ridgely, Maryland. This suburb of Cumberland was named after the Reverend Greenbury W. Ridgely, a law partner of Henry Clay. The first attempt to lay out the town was during a land promotion scheme that failed in 1867, but the plan was later revitalized and put into effect.

Cumberland was a major Potomac port where flat-bottomed barges loaded with the fruits, grain and coal of the Ohio Valley left to float downstream to Washington, D.C. Cumberland lies at the eastern foot of the Appalachian Plateau surrounded by mountaintops. Cumberland's altitude is 641 feet above sea level, yet mountains, which rise up to 2,300 feet above sea level around the town, surround it. Thomas Beall founded Cumberland near the point where Wills Creek cuts a pathway through the mountain and enters the Potomac. Will Rogers once described the town as a city built between two railroad tracks.

Cumberland, as we had discovered earlier in our trip, was the city where the C&O Canal ends. We drove back to the Cumberland Train Station museum and found that the C&O Canal portion of the museum was open and staffed by a very informative National Park Service ranger. It was still early morning but the museum was open and we were the only customers. The Park Service ranger we met inside the museum was so glad to have someone to talk to that she began reciting historical trivia from memory. She kept me listening until I couldn't absorb any more. Tom had quietly slipped away when she began talking and had found safe refuge behind his camera. He was busy taking photographs of the area while I began storing up on research material.

The C&O Canal extends 185 miles from Cumberland to Washington, D.C. Construction of the C&O Canal began on July 4th, 1828, with President John Quincy Adams turning the first shovel of earth. In Georgetown on Wisconsin Avenue next to the canal there is a nondescript obelisk commemorating this event.

On that same day in 1828, Charles Carroll, a signer of the Declaration of Independence, turned the first shovel of dirt in Baltimore to begin construction of the Baltimore and Ohio Railroad. Although not realized then, the canal and the railroad would fight over the same trade. The entire length of the canal was not completed until 1850. The canal, finished first, prospered until the railroad, then capable of hauling more loads and providing faster, cheaper transportation, sounded the death knell for the canal system. Today, I was standing inside a building that was once a train depot and was now the C&O Canal Museum. That was ironic enough for me to search out Tom and tell him what I thought was so funny.

Looking out the window of the museum, I caught a glimpse of Tom photographing Wills Creek as it flowed past us and into the Potomac. The weather had gotten noticeably colder. I bundled up and went out to find Tom. We walked downstream along Wills Creek and followed the signs to the origin of the C&O Canal and its last mile marker - 184.5 miles.

"Y'know," I said, "This mile marker should be the 0 mile marker instead of the 184.5 mile marker.

It should show the beginning of the canal rather than the end." Tom hid himself behind his camera.

The view of the Cumberland church spires pointing toward the heavens, the flowing river below, and the water trapped between flood control walls of concrete, makes for an enjoyable walk along this portion of the river.

It was the canal that allowed these barges to move more safely. The barges ran parallel with the Potomac and used its waters to float past the more dangerous points at Harpers Ferry, Seneca Rapids and Great Falls.

Just south of Cumberland, the Potomac waters of the North Branch waters twist and turn as if fighting to maintain their northerly momentum. Finally, taking in the southern flowing waters of Evitts River and Lake Gordon from Pennsylvania, the river rounds the Cumberland Municipal Airport. It twists again and begins heading east where it passes Spring Gap, West Virginia and Oldtown, Maryland. These towns are connected by one of only two toll bridges crossing the Potomac. The other is the Route 301 Bridge, which is the last bridge to cross the Potomac before the waters flow into the Chesapeake Bay. We put our inflatable boat in the water at Cumberland.

An inflatable boat was the most desirable boat for us to travel in, as we could transport it easily in the back of the camper. Inflating such a boat is easy. We would run a hose from a SCUBA tank filled with compressed air to the various connections on the boat. Within a few minutes we had maritime transportation at our disposal. In the days to come we would sometimes travel in two cars, and pre-stage one at the site we expected to reach by the end of our trip for that day. The other car would carry the boat and essentials packed in it. When the boat was inflated and filled with cameras, food, and other necessities, we would lock the car and begin our trip. At the end, we would pack up the first car we had pre-staged and drive back to recover the other car. Not the most efficient method, but it worked all right for us.

Although we put the boat in the water at Cumberland just downstream from Wills Creek and from the waterfall under the Route 28 Bridge, we were still not officially on what is called the Potomac River. We were still on the North Branch of the Potomac. On this trip we would soon see the South Branch Potomac flowing out the Allegheny Mountains just upstream from Paw Paw, West Virginia. The confluence of these two branches is where the Potomac River officially begins. Our next stop today would be at Paw Paw, West Virginia.

We planned to start the engine and speed toward the confluence of the two river branches, but the water appeared to be moving us fast enough. Tom simply steered the boat while I sat back to watch the passing scenery. The first thing that almost immediately caught our attention was the way the two banks of the river appeared to converge together just beyond a train trestle ahead of us. It seemed from where we were that the two shorelines narrowed and met; the water just stops flowing; even looking like it could be falling into a bottomless pit. As we pulled closer, the 50-foot width between shorelines dropped to about

10 feet; Tom started the engine in case we were about to enter some wicked whitewater.

We entered the narrow opening and the tree limbs stretching across the river from each shore were almost touching each other. The whitewater we feared never happened. We continued to float around to our left and Tom, sensing little need for the engine, shut it off. The noise of the engine was reverberating in our ears. As it diminished, we both began to hear the sound of something like distant thunder with a slightly higher pitch. Tom and I were twisting our heads back and forth like radar trying to tune in and locate the source of the noise. It sounded like it was coming either directly in front of us or slightly to our right. As we were turning our heads, our eyes met and the expression on our faces must have read the same thing. We were both imagining that the noise we heard was the thunder of an upcoming waterfall. Tom had even reached back to crank up the engine again. What we both realized at almost the same instant was that the noise was now coming from above our heads and over to our right. It was the sound of an aircraft engine; and the chart showed that the aircraft was preparing to take off from Cumberland Airport. We just looked at each other and wondered what we were going to dream up next. We floated completely around the airport and at one point our own mode of maritime transportation floated directly between the air transportation at Cumberland Airport to our right and the train transportation to our left. Past the trains was Route 51 filled with passing cars. We hit a small patch of whitewater that brought our attention back to our own form of transportation. We made a sharp turn to our right and passed under another small bridge. We continued to hear aircraft engines coming from the airport, but they slowly slipped away from us as we began moving away from the area.

We came upon some interesting phenomena over the next few miles. The first was when the water came to a 'T'. The North Branch of the Potomac stopped flowing straight and made an abrupt 90-degree turn to the left. There was nothing but low lying farmland in front of us. It didn't seem possible that Mother Nature would have turned the river 90 degrees to the left for no reason. There was another stream flowing past us from right to left, as if it were the making the top of the letter 'T'. Once the North Branch of the Potomac turned to flow into this other branch, it should have taken on the name of that branch. The water was still called the Potomac. The only other time we saw this happen was at Harpers Ferry where the 'T' this time was the Potomac and the Shenandoah Rivers. Again, as the Potomac reached the top of the 'T' and turned 90 degrees to the left to converge with the Shenandoah River, which was crossing along the top of the 'T' from right to left, one would assume the name of the river would change to the Shenandoah River. As you know, the Potomac keeps its name all the way to where it flows into the Chesapeake Bay. Tom drew the analogy first.

"You know," he said, "if you were driving a car along a road that ended at a 'T', and then took a left onto the road running across the top of the 'T', the name of the road you were on would change. That sure doesn't happen here."

We made the turn and remained on the Potomac. We passed under another bridge and began following the river as it continued to wind back and forth through the valley. At one point we noticed a second anomaly. Tom and I had both heard the saying that there is no such thing as a straight line to Mother Nature. Yet throughout the normally winding river, we would sometimes float through areas that were so straight you would swear they were man-made trenches that the river was flowing through. We were on such a stretch now, and a fork in the river loomed straight ahead.

We took the left fork of the river around the island, but before we met the right fork again we came across another fork. This time we took the right fork to make sure we would meet the right fork from our previous selection. The main body of water formed up again and we continued our downstream run. It was growing late so Tom kicked in the engine and we headed downstream at a faster pace. After a few more turns in the river we came across a large bridge crossing a river to our right. Behind the bridge were the remains of another bridge that appeared to have been washed away by a flood some years ago. What we were seeing was the South Branch of the Potomac flowing into the North Branch of the Potomac. We had reached a major point of our trip - we were finally on the Potomac River.

Although we did not jump out of our boat with excitement upon reaching this confluence, I found it difficult to have spent so much time writing about the North Branch of the Potomac without writing something about the South Branch. So before continuing our Potomac journey downstream to Paw

Paw, it only seems fair to freeze time and mentally jump to the beginning of the South Branch for a short tour.

Many sources claim that the length of the Potomac is nearly 400 miles. Others state a more precise 383 miles. Either length is claimed as the distance from the Fairfax Stone on the North Branch of the Potomac to Point Lookout. Not added to this mileage figure, of course, are all the tributaries that flow into the Potomac. An important tributary that we also explored was the South Branch of the Potomac River.

As the North Branch has its headwaters, so too does the South Branch. The South Branch begins draining from land at Hightown, Virginia. The town's more advertised claim-to-fame is having "The Highest Post Office In The State" in elevation above sea level, 3,123 feet. Hightown is in Highland County, an area affectionately called "Little Switzerland of America" by the locals because this county has the highest mean altitude of Virginia's counties. The farmland where the South Branch of the Potomac begins is at Jacob Hevener's Farm called "Dividing Waters" Farm - where rainwater running off the farm in a northerly direction flows into the South Branch of the Potomac on the North side of Rt. 250 while water running off the farm in a southerly direction eventually flows into the James River on the South side of Rt. 250. They meet again in the Chesapeake Bay at Norfolk, Virginia, just before flowing into the Atlantic Ocean. The South Branch of the Potomac makes a struggling effort to seep out of the ground at Dividing Waters Farms, but during the hot summer months these springs dry up. A few miles further

down the hill, though, enough water is still perking out of the mountain to form a continuous stream.

The South Branch of the Potomac begins it downstream journey by running between the crests of the Allegheny and Appalachian Mountains. The stream flows in a north-northeast direction toward the West Virginia town of Moyers. It flows past the West Virginia towns of Franklin and Upper Tract, through the Spruce Knob-Seneca Rocks National Recreation Area, and past Petersburg, Moorefield, Old Fields, and Romney before merging with the North Branch of the Potomac. Romney was the site of 56 minor battles between the North and the South during the Civil War. It is also near Romney where the North and South branches of the Potomac River merge.

When we passed the South Branch tributary and drifted into the official Potomac River, we noticed ourselves pushed slightly to the right. It is unclear on how much water is added to the Potomac by the South Branch, but we almost immediately hit whitewater that accelerated our downstream journey. Soon we passed the southern flowing waters of Maryland's Maple River as it entered the Potomac. We then floated past the first official Potomac River town and the first official Potomac River bridge—at Paw Paw, West Virginia.

From the water, the only thing that told us that we had reached Paw Paw was that the bridge we passed under was marked on the topographic map. On the one bank was West Virginia; on the other was Maryland.

"Tom," I asked, "How are you going to paint a quaint town like Paw Paw nestled along the banks of the Potomac when you can't even see any of the town from the water in the first place?"

It was a question we asked ourselves repeatedly as we passed by many more towns built too far up the bank to see. Later we figured out the reason why these towns did that: flood control.

We stayed content with the view of the Paw Paw Bridge, in which a tree, uprooted during a recent flood, had drifted downstream and locked itself around the structure. It stranded itself high and dry on a flat portion of the bridge concrete support, some 4 feet above our heads as we drifted under it. Other large trunks, with roots looking like Medusa's head of snakes, lay along the banks. The banks beneath both sides of the Paw Paw Bridge were layered with rocks placed there by man. A huge metal net, looking like a fisherman's net, was lying on top of the rocks, spiked into place between the rocks. The net was there to keep these rocks from being pushed away from the bridge's foundation. It was a quiet reminder of the fury of the waters. Watermarks staining the concrete bridge went higher up the spans than where we could reach as we floated past. Night was approaching as we pulled the inflatable boat out of the water at Paw Paw National Park and called it a day.

Later that evening a small portion of the river had flooded from some overnight rains and overflowed its banks. The Allegheny County Commission signed an emergency order declaring portions of the county a disaster area; some homes and businesses had been damaged severely. These flash floods are extremely dangerous. Here many streams had jumped their banks, flooded basements and first floors of houses with up to 8 feet of mud, and then receded - all in a matter of 20 minutes. The water in the swollen streams was pouring into the Potomac, and the river was as brown and frothy as chocolate milk and flowing very quickly. We had planned to put our inflatable back into the water, but the park rangers issued a small craft warning and told us that they didn't want to see any more people and their boats on the river until it returned to normal.

Hours later the river was still chocolate-brown in color and the current was making tiny whirlpools in the high, fast moving water. We had just about decided that this was going to be a wasted day when a group of Boy Scouts and their adult leaders showed up with a truck. The truck was towing a rack of nearly 20 canoes. Three canoes went into the water and a few of the adults took off downstream to test the conditions. The truck drove off to pick them up and bring them back. An hour later they were back saying that it was a good run and telling the Scouts to get their canoes in the water.

Following their lead, we pulled our inflatable out of the camper around noon, hooked up a bottle of compressed air, and had the boat inflated and in the water in 15 minutes. Loading it with an outboard motor, gas tank, food, cameras, film, topographic maps, a bailing bucket, and ourselves, we settled down to a leisurely tour of the West Virginia and Maryland countryside. Since we did not pre-stage a car further downstream and lacked a way of getting back if the motor conked out on us or if we ran out of gas, we decided to go upstream first. That way if anything happened we could simply drift back to our starting position.

With the Potomac waters pushing against us at a pace that surprised us, we soon discovered that this was not going to be a trip without some risk. It was normal to have only inches of clearance between the bottom of our boat and the riverbed along portions of the upper Potomac. Today we had about four feet of water. Even so, we still felt things brushing against the bottom of the boat. Experienced boaters call these "witches fingers." With the inflatable's small motor, it was apparent that we were not going to go anywhere very far or fast. At times the motor would be at full throttle and yet we would come to a complete stop. The outboard motor was doing fine for now, but the current was about to win out. We figured it wouldn't take us long to travel some distance upstream from where we launched the boat. An hour later we had passed under a railroad bridge and the Paw Paw Bridge that crossed the Potomac. The uprooted tree that we had seen on our first trip wrapped around a Paw Paw Bridge support was still there, but this time we were level with it. After motoring a few hundred yards past the bridge, we gave up and turned around. It took us 15 minutes to get back to where we launched. We would eventually come back to Paw Paw on four separate occasions to experience this portion of the river and walk along the C&O Canal.

On one later trip, after the floodwaters had receded, we repeated our trip upstream and saw that the tree we had seen on the bridge support was gone.

Another reason for visiting the area so often was to visit the Paw Paw Tunnel.

The Paw Paw Tunnel is an interesting highlight along the C&O Canal. This tunnel is 3,118 feet in length, excavated through solid rock, and was by far the canal's most ambitious project. Here the water of the Potomac travels three-fifths of a mile before rejoining the river, which had been twisting and turning for nearly seven miles around the mountain through which the tunnel passed.

Exiting the tunnel at the far end, we continued walking along the right side of the hollow on a wooden walkway, waiting to meet the Potomac waters again. Remembering we had to walk back, we gave up and returned to walk through the tunnel again. It surprised us that our eyes, after becoming accustomed to the darkness of the tunnel, found the light at the end of the tunnel appeared so close. We walked and walked but the light streaming in the door at the end of the tunnel still looked just as far away. Our dilated eyes had tired from the strain, the sun was getting near the western horizon, and the tunnel exit seemed to stay just beyond our reach; our minds were playing tricks on us. Finally, emerging into the last sunlight of the day, we were temporarily blinded until our pupils returned to normal. There we rested at a picnic table and watched the brown Potomac waters flow by.

Back at the water's edge and standing on the concrete pier, Tom and I surveyed the river downstream and noticed that eddies and riffles were appearing where the natural flow of the water was disrupted by rocks jutting up from the river bottom. Many rocks were not high enough to break the surface. We listened quietly to the noise the water was making, and saw the areas where the moving water dropped over wide stretches of nearly exposed rock - whitewater mini-rapids. We were about to enter an area called Paw Paw Bends. It was these riffles and the twisting, turning bends that convinced the management of the C&O Canal to dig the tunnel. Now we were going to see first-hand why they had chosen to build the tunnel here.

I turned to Tom, who appeared not the least bit concerned. That worried me, as the adrenaline began to seep into my veins, making my heart pump just a little more strongly. Tom and I are opposites in many ways, which may be why we have been friends for so long. Had we both had the same interests over the years, we probably would both be dead by now. I am glad he finally got married after 33 years as a bachelor; I have turned over the reins of temperance to his wife, and wished her good luck.

Now I look back at Tom in the inflatable and I see him with that look of not having a care in the world. He knew that no matter what happened to us, we would walk away from it. This time it was literal because the stream wasn't any deeper than about three feet at any point we had been so far. If we tipped over we would just walk to the shore.

While Tom studied the riffles and different colors of the water, I was thinking about how we could manage to gather up all our gear if we flipped over. I remembered something I had read before - don't hang on to the downstream side of the overturned boat. If you do you will find yourself a poor substitute for a cushion when the current pushes the boat and you up against an outcropping of rock. I concluded the same held true for the inflatable we had with us this time, a flat bottom inflatable with a small engine hanging off the stern. We pushed off from the shoreline with our oars and begin drifting toward the noise of riffles and into Paw Paw Bends.

We were quiet as we passed by trees toppled over during the recent floods. They were all underwater the last time we were here. Their trunks, all in a row pointing downstream, lay dead and rotting on Bevan Bend, covered in dried mud and parched by the sun. Although we heard many birds in the surrounding area, we saw none perched on the dead branches of those to our right. Maintaining equal distance between both banks, hoping that was the deepest portion of the river, we turned toward our right and began our drift downstream. We passed under another Western Maryland Railroad bridge with the left bank of the Potomac climbing higher than the right. After crossing right to left, the railroad tracks come off the bridge and into Kesler Tunnel.

Tom broke the quiet. "I wonder what a train sounds like inside a tunnel?"

We continued downstream before Tom got the chance to push ashore and climb into the tunnel to answer his question. To our left, the stream of water from Big Run, although there is nothing big about it, gurgles into the Potomac. Ahead, the steep cliff rising to our left diminishes while the cliff on our right begins to sharpen its angle. We "read" the river and determined that the cliffs could also tell us how the river is about to bend. It did and we continued our drifting downstream. The water is cold as we reach over and stick our fingers into it.

Tom's oar was used as a rudder to keep the boat parallel with the riverbanks. We saw the cliff to our left and anticipated another bend of the river, this time to our right. As we drift around the bend, we were surprised to see another railroad bridge stretch across the river. The Western Maryland, cutting a more straight line through the mountains than the river, runs across each river bend, alternately passing through Maryland, West Virginia, Maryland, West Virginia, etc.

Tom caught the anomaly. "How did we miss the Western Maryland on its last cut? Surely we should have seen another bridge sending it back to West Virginia before we saw it again coming out of West Virginia and into Maryland? Where exactly did that tunnel go, anyway?"

I thought that maybe we should have stopped and explored that railroad tunnel back a couple of miles. I'm glad I didn't say that aloud, because here was another railroad bridge whose tracks also led into another tunnel. This time it wasn't the Western Maryland but the Baltimore and Ohio Railroad. Having just run through the middle of Paw Paw, the tracks popped out of Carothers Tunnel, ran along the right bank of the Potomac, crossed the bridge we were now drifting under, and back into another tunnel—Graham Tunnel. We kept drifting.

We again drifted around a bend, this time to our left, noticing the streams on our right called Steer

Run and Little Steer Run, (although I couldn't tell their difference from the rate of water flow, but each was adding some more water into the Potomac). More water flowed into the river from the right—that from Shambaugh Hollow. Most of the water from the streams on our right had been flowing down from the West Virginian Cacapon Hills. The water from the few streams to our left where flowing down from the Maryland Sorrell and Anthony Ridges.

Then it was more water from Springs Hollow and Gross Hollow, back under a B&O Railroad bridge, and Station Hollow, where, less than a mile later, after choosing the wider path of water when we came to a split in the river, we again met another Western Maryland railroad bridge.

Our rate of drift noticeably increased as the width of the Potomac sharply decreased. Anywhere along the river thus far we could have tossed a rock out of the inflatable and hit either shore. Here we were even closer. We were passing an unnamed island in the Potomac, one of many that we would pass. For this one we had made the right decision on what side to go around. Tom had the river make the decision for us. With our inflatable boat pretty much in the middle of the Potomac, we drifted and Tom took the oar/rudder out of the water. A larger amount of water would either be flowing to the left or right of the island. By drifting we would be sucked down the channel where most of the water is also going. Nature agreed with Tom, for as we passed the island and the two separated streams of the Potomac merged, we looked back upstream into the channel we did not take. It was smaller than what we had just passed through. Not bad, I thought. Then I started thinking about the one time where the river would push us over the falls instead of taking us around the smaller but quieter channel. It would be my luck. Tom broke the silence:

"What I just did," Tom said, "was the same principle that 'cavers' and cave-divers take."

Often a "caver" will stop at a divergence of two underground paths and pick the one where the wind is predominantly blowing. An underwater cave diver, in a cave where the water flows out, will usually remain still and let the current pull him into the correct channel.

After the two passages merged back into one Potomac, a stream appeared on the left, Sandy Flat Hollow. Finally, the C&O Canal reappeared out of the mountain, having taken the short cut through the Paw Paw Tunnel. The C&O Canal would now follow parallel to the river until its end at Georgetown in the District of Columbia. Another curve to our right, past another Gross Hollow, Twigg Hollow, and again we drifted under a Western Maryland Railroad bridge. A good-sized stream, Roby Hollow, was dumping more water into the Potomac on our left just past the bridge. The Potomac was getting a little deeper, but not much wider.

I'm sure the compass I had attached to my coat was having fits. Its magnetized needle had followed the path of the Potomac from its origin at the Fairfax Stone and had registered nearly every direction of the compass since then. Very early during this journey we had correctly assumed that this was going to be a quiet portion of the river - great for drifting and talking about the book. We were right, and it sure was relaxing. It wasn't very long before Tom and I felt like we were going crazy. We couldn't even tune in a radio station much less get a weather report. We were drifting in a dead zone. At points along the drifting, away from the railroad trestles and tracks, it would have been impossible to prove that we were even in the 20th Century. Drifting in the Potomac in these mountains, we could have gone back in time 2 million years and probably not known the difference. Rounding a bend, we could have drifted past prehistoric man hiding behind ferns and we would have never known it. Now, in the 20th Century, we were drifting around another bend, noticing more water flowing into the Potomac from the right-hand shoreline. On the chart I read the names of Hansrote Hollow, Larrys Hollow, Freestone Hollow, and Spring Hollow, all flowing down from Purslane Mountain. Then we reached Randolph Tunnel. The temperature dropped as the sun began playing through the upper trees along the top of the ridges. Tom kicked in the Evinrude and we headed back upstream to Paw Paw.

CHAPTER 2

From Paw Paw, West Virginia, to Harpers Ferry, West Virginia

We launched the inflatable at the Fifteen Mile Creek C&O Canal Park at Little Orleans, Maryland. A quick look around before we departed revealed an aqueduct taking the C&O Canal waters across Fifteen Mile Creek that was feeding into the Potomac. The creek is 15 miles from Oldtown and 15 miles from Hancock, a fact that held some significance in the days of the old trails. Little Orleans first appeared on a map dated 1866 and was named for a city in France. A few people were sitting on folding chairs, throwing their fishing lines into the creek. There were also two parked cars with empty boat trailers attached to them, although we never saw any boats on the Potomac until we neared Hancock.

We walked back to the road to talk to some Boy Scouts who were setting up camp along the C&O Canal. They said that they had paddled their canoes down this stretch of river before and that the only excitement this stretch had to offer was a slight whitewater rapid at the remains of a dam called Feeder Dam Number 6. The river had eventually succeeded in wiping out this dam that was used to siphon water off the Potomac and into the C&O Canal. One Scout claimed that he once tipped over his canoe on purpose when he hit the whitewater. He said it was a real hot day and he wanted to cool off. He went on to say that we shouldn't have any problems at all. Most Scouts, they said, canoe this stretch as an introduction to the river. The Scouts said we wouldn't have to concentrate on maneuvering as much as just watching what was happening around us.

We loaded up the boat and pushed off from the boat ramp. We first rowed upstream for about 50 feet before being caught by the current and turned around to be sent downstream. The engine would be used on this trip only if we found ourselves running late.

The Scouts were correct about the ease with which this stretch of river ran, with just a couple of surprises awaiting us. Almost immediately, we found the current pushing us toward the right of the river, where we guessed it must be deeper. As we floated over to the right we found that the river was also trying to push us ashore on some low-lying mudbanks. This area would be underwater even during a minor flood, but for now the river seemed content on pushing whatever was in the river onto the mud. There were small tree trunks and some trash; all waiting for the eventual floodwaters that would free them from the low-lying mudbank and push them further downstream. We didn't have the time to wait until the next flood. The oars came back out and we rowed our way out into the left-to-center area of the river.

We soon came across another mudbank sticking out from the left of the river. A stream that was pushing its silt out into the river created this one. We found it interesting that the river was not, in turn, pushing this accumulated silt further downstream. The silt and mud stretched across nearly half the width of the Potomac. This got Tom and I into a discussion about farmers and how rain would catch the topsoil on a recently plowed field and sweep it into the nearby streams. The soil would, in turn, sweep down into the larger streams and rivers. Not only would the topsoil go downstream, but also any fertilizers residing in the topsoil also would be washed downstream. The fertilizers would concentrate in the river in enough proportion to support the growth of algae. This algae growth would suck all the oxygen content out of a water causing massive fish kills. This led us into a discussion of natural fertilizers and into a discussion on the cost of chemical fertilizers versus natural fertilizers. The discussion had stopped when we hit the town of Great Cacapon. Ahead of us were similar patches of land jutting out from the shore straight into the river, just below where a stream was pouring out into the river. One river to our right, the Cacapon River, was wide enough at its mouth to support two bridges. Just downstream from this area we hit a small amount of white water to our left. After passing that we then looked like we were going to be swallowed up by a huge mountain looming up into the sky in front of us.

The landscape around the mountain looked vaguely familiar. As we slowly began to loop around to our left, we scanned the ridgeline and saw something that attracted our attention. It was an area that had been cleared away from the face of the mountain, like where sightseers would stop and take pictures. Which is why it looked familiar, because we once pulled our cars over on Route 9 to look out over the Potomac from that clearing. The clearing is called Prospect Peak and from that clearing, which overlooks the Potomac and Great Cacapon Valleys, you can see West Virginia, Pennsylvania and Maryland. The

National Geographic Magazine rated this scene among America's outstanding beauty spots.

Back on the river, we saw ahead of us what appeared to be the remains of the dam that the Scouts had talked about earlier. We shifted toward the left and passed through an opening in the dam with little problem, except that the inflatable was slightly wider than a canoe and it protested a bit getting through the opening. In front of us was another decision to make. An island appeared in the middle of the river and the decision was made to run to the left. Floating to the left, we immediately had another choice to make: catch the whitewater that had appeared to our left or hug the island to our right. We chose to go right and bypass the whitewater, which was a good idea because I had felt something wet beneath me. The inflatable was filling up with water and my tennis shoes were soaking up some of that water.

We did a quick check of the inflatable's individual cells that held air, and none of them appeared to be losing any. The only conclusion left was that we had caught the bottom of the boat on something that had ripped a small hole in the material beneath the wooden boards. The boat uses five wooden decking boards that slide into each other and cover the entire bottom of the boat, giving the boat its stability. Without the boards the two ends of the boat would rise upwards and push Tom and I into the center of the inflatable boat like a sandwich. We steered to the Maryland shoreline, jumped ashore and pulled the boat up out of the water. We took everything out of the boat and then flipped it over to inspect the damage. A tear looking like the letter L and about one-inch in length along each side of the L was what drove us ashore. Using a bicycle tube patch kit, Tom dried off the surface, applied the adhesive, and stuck on patches to both sides of the tear. We then sat back and had a leisurely lunch of peanut butter and jelly sandwiches and soft drinks.

We were soon back in the water and within a few minutes found ourselves making a sharp turn to our left. Then we made a turn to our right and almost immediately heard the distinct sound of a large outboard motor. As we rounded that last turn we spotted a powerboat that had turned around in the river in front of us and was now heading back downstream. The boat's wake, while dissipated, was felt as it passed under our boat. To our right a camper had pitched a tent along the West Virginia bank of the river. We were beginning to see signs of civilization. Ahead of us was Hancock's Route 522 Bridge crossing the Potomac. This was the first passenger car-carrying bridge to cross the Potomac since Paw Paw. We passed under the bridge and saw the graffiti spray-painted on the bridge's concrete support beams. Tom and I talked about how little graffiti had changed since the days we were in high school, and probably since the days our parents had attended high school. The kids today still paint "Class of ..." and "John and Debbie XXX" on concrete bridge supports.

We moved over to our left, passed Little Tonoloway Creek, and immediately pulled up onto the steep boat ramp. We pulled the boat ashore and moved it off to the side. The people in the bassboat that had come up behind us wanted to get their boat onto the trailer that was backed down on the ramp. We were back in Hancock, sitting in the Little Tonoloway C&O Canal Park parking lot where we had earlier left the other car. Our thoughts were slowly gravitating away from the river and toward something to eat. We packed up and soon found ourselves enjoying an early dinner at the Hancock Crab House. The Scouts at Little Orleans were correct calling this an uneventful section of the river. Of interest, though, is the fact that the Potomac makes its most northerly bend here, trimming the width of Maryland to two miles. It is believed that the town of Hancock was named for Joseph Hancock who settled here in 1749.

We left the Little Tonoloway C&O Canal Park at Hancock and headed for Williamsport. We got an early start, but then had to inflate and push the boat into the water from the side of the ramp. There were several cars lined up ready to back their boats into the water when we had arrived to do the same. Once in the water Tom started the engine and we began moving downstream. Other boats were already in the water, some speeding by and throwing "rooster tails" of water up behind them as they sped by.

We reached a fork in the river formed by another island, and the boat traffic died down. We took the larger fork but still found a shallow mud bank to our right hugging the island. We assumed these boats were not passing through this area because of the shallowness of the river. Our boat, only taking a couple of inches of draft, alleviated our worry. As we passed by this island, we noticed that it looked lopsided for some reason. I mentioned it to Tom who then brought to my attention that all the tall trees on the islands were located on the downstream side, while all the low-lying bush and undergrowth were located on the upstream side. We could only conclude that floods were still significant enough through this area to have taken out the trees along the upstream half of the island. We figured that the torrential waters from each successive flood were knocking down the trees as the island slowly eroded from the floodwaters. These trees looked like they had been there for many years, yet we've seen larger tree trunks floating downstream in the river, torn out with their roots by the floodwaters.

We reached Little Pool, Maryland, but never saw the small lake from the Potomac. We did reach another island, though, but this one looked man-made. While the Potomac flowed mostly to its left, which was the path we took, the right-hand side of the fork looked like it was dug out in a straight line. We figured there probably would be a mill close by this smaller stream that used a waterwheel to turn its millstone. We peered down the small inlet and saw nothing but trees lining both sides. Passing this island, we reached another fork in the river and took the right side. We went in that direction because we saw something in the distance rising out of the river that made us very curious. As we approached it, we soon identified it as the ruins of a bridge now long forgotten. We had reached Big Pool, Maryland, by chart, but as with Little Pool, we didn't see either the town or the pool of water from where they got their name. Both Little and Big Pool, Maryland, came into existence with the building of the C&O

Canal. The canal passed through these pieces of low swampy land, and these swamps immediately filled with water up to the canal level, forming the pools. Big Pool was once over 700 feet wide and abounded in fish and waterfowl.

We then came upon a sharp turn in the river as it bent toward the left, reminding us that we had traveled in a fairly straight line for some 10 miles since leaving Hancock. We passed Back Creek flowing into the Potomac from the West Virginia side and came across another sharp bend to our left. Boats immediately surrounded us. If there was a "No Wake" zone around this portion of the river, it couldn't be found.

These were the largest boats we had seen on the river so far. You would normally see these types of boats in the deeper tidal areas of the Potomac downstream from Georgetown. They were mostly zooming upstream, killing their engines, and then drifting downstream with everyone's fishing lines dropping into the water.

We spotted a large outcropping of rock some 50 feet wide and 20 to 30 feet high. This signified the end to this portion of the river and a most welcome break for us as we approached the McCoys Ferry C&O Canal boat ramp. We approached the ramp on our left and saw that this ramp was built pointing downstream. Every other ramp we had used had been pointing slightly upstream. If you have ever loaded or unloaded a boat from a trailer into a current, you realize why it is difficult to do so when the ramp is pointing downstream. As you unload it, the boat tends to catch the current and begin drifting downstream before you have a chance to unsnap the safety and winch lines. This also means that someone should be onboard the boat as it floats off the trailer and begins drifting, ready to start the engine and return. When loading the boat you have to keep the engine engaged and running until you hook on the safety or winch line. If the ramp was facing upstream, you could disengage the engine much earlier and drift down into the trailer, possibly saving your engine propeller from striking something in the shallow waters. In our case, we had a choice to make. We could start up the engine and hope that we didn't catch the prop on the concrete ramp or break out the oars and paddle our way like crazy back upstream to the ramp. Neither choice was liked, so we drifted past the ramp and edged in close to the bank. I jumped ashore from the front of the boat with our towline and walked the boat and Tom back to the ramp. Twice I had to slip the towline around trees that were growing along the bank. Tom had to remain in the boat in case the towline slipped from my hands and allowed the boat to drift away.

It was here at the McCoys Ferry C&O Canal aqueduct where, on May 23rd, 1861, Confederates attempting to capture the ferryboat at McCoys Landing were driven off by a single guard. Also here, on October 10, 1862, General J.E.B. Stuart crossed the Potomac on his second ride around McClellan's army.

We went back to our small inflatable to continue downstream. Before we put the boat back in the water two huge outboard engines broke the relative silence. We saw two powerboats turning around in sharp circles, hitting each other's wake and trying to get airborne. The game then broke off and these two boats roared back upstream to another section of the river, their wakes hitting both the Maryland and West Virginia shorelines. We were glad we weren't anywhere on the river close to them, but those speedboats were the exception rather than the rule. Along this part of the Potomac, bassboats are the boat of choice. A bassboat is a flat but wide-bottomed aluminum boat that sits low in the water band is still large enough to handle a good-sized engine hanging off the stern. Bassboats were everywhere.

The Potomac then bent around to the right and back to the left. Through the openings in the trees along the right side of the river we saw houses down almost to the water's edge. There were floating piers and boat ramps all along the West Virginia side. Then it was back sharply to the right before the Potomac settled down and aimed itself right for Feeder Dam Number 5. The Feeder Dam was used to divert water off the Potomac and into the C&O Canal. It appeared this dam was now being used to siphon water off the river for use as the town's supply of drinking water. Just before we pulled the boat out of the water on the Maryland side, we saw more boats and our first water-skier.

With the boat out of the water, we walked up a small hill to view the dam. We were warned about this one and it was not one to try going over. From the top of the viewing area, the rock wall was filled with some people fishing and others just relaxing. Some fishing lines were in the water above the dam and some were below. Two bassboats and their passengers lurked in the waters below the dam, in the lee of an island, with their lines stretched out into the water.

Tom and I took a deep breath and went to complete the final section of river on this trip. We dragged the boat down the hill past the dam and reentered the water. We were surrounded by a multitude of small islands. These were soon behind us, the smaller islands appearing to coalesce into larger ones. We then came across a fork in the river with a large island directly in front of us. We went to the left of the island, but the side we picked began to decrease in width. We had an opportunity to change sides when an opening appeared between two islands. The boat didn't fit and it was too shallow, so we got out and pulled it with us. Once on the other side of the island we saw that this side was where most of the Potomac waters had gone. Ahead of us were the remains of another bridge, with only its supports left, jutting out of the water and along both shorelines.

The river then looped left and right and we continued drifting. A boat passed us heading upstream but didn't give us any notice. We drifted past Duck Island and then another unnamed island. The islands were becoming commonplace and we began to wonder when this section of the river was going to be over.

We were approaching a state of mind commonly associated with daydreaming. We were becoming mesmerized, or hypnotized, by the unchanging scenery and the slowness of the river. We were seeing nothing but miles of shoreline choked with trees and undergrowth. Our minds were vegetating with every passing mile. What we feared would happen was happening; we were becoming complacent about the surroundings and oblivious to what lay ahead. Some

would have said they had gotten down to enjoying the river; for Tom and me, it was excruciatingly painful to sit and do little but watch the shoreline. As we moved downstream, I fiddled with the topographic map.

"Hey Tom," I said sleepily, after looking at the map and visualizing what was coming up, "we have a photo opportunity coming up."

"Just great," Tom replied.

The river was taking its toll on us. Any other time we would be discussing what lens we were using on our cameras, the film speed we were using, the best angle to shoot from, if we should go ashore, and dozens of other questions. Now we were hard-pressed to work up any enthusiasm to use our cameras for what lay ahead.

Tom and I were taught to use cameras in two different ways. Yet, when we both approach a subject and are both looking through our respective lenses, we both click the shutter at nearly the same time. My formal photography schooling came from the University of Kansas, as did Tom's. While working my way through a Bachelor of Science degree at the William Allen White School of Journalism, the photography classes I took dealt with photojournalism. I was taught to tell a complete story with one photograph. Even today, while peering through my Through-The-Lens viewfinder, I move the field of vision around until I capture just the story I want to tell. Tom, with a Bachelor of Arts degree in Theater Design, becomes more interested in capturing moods, patterns and colors. Our basic schooling is still there, like remembering the rule of thirds and depth of field, but we look at things we are about to take a picture of differently. Yet it's funny how we seem to take pictures almost simultaneously.

"C'mon Tom," I insisted, "the Conococheague River is coming up and the C&O Canal goes over the river in another aqueduct. It says here 'the aqueduct is an example of artistry in limestone; that it was built by Irish immigrant laborers skilled in the art of stonemasonry.' It should look pretty good and we can shoot it as we drift by."

Tom began to move and he went reaching for his camera bag. "Now that does sound like something interesting."

"Williamsport and the aqueduct are at the same spot" I continued. "The map shows River Front Park with a boat ramp right near the bridge that crosses the Potomac."

We approached the convergence of the Potomac and Conococheague with cameras in hand; our minds focused on the perfect shot of the aqueduct with its reflection in the water. We were going to use the trees along the shoreline as a frame, and possibly while some joggers were running across the aqueduct to establish the relative size of the aqueduct. Tom and I were clicking our cameras at the same time, which always gives me that feeling that something must be going right. We were, independent of each other, lining up the same shots and taking nearly the same photograph. I ran out of film, so I put my camera down and picked up my brochure of the area. I knew we were going to float beneath the Route 11 Bridge before going ashore, so I read from the brochure that the bridge we were coming to was a Bollman Steel

Truss bridge built in 1879. It is only one of two such structures left standing in the United States. That's when I heard Tom say "Oops."

Now normally a person saying "Oops" means something insignificant, like they dropped their pen on the floor or forgot to pick up their dry cleaning. When Tom says "Oops" I usually dive for cover. There are certain people in certain situations where you do not want to hear them say "Oops." For example, while you're on the operating table. I once read a summary report of fatal aircraft accidents. The thing that caught my attention was that the pilots would usually start whistling a tune right before the crash. In other cases, the pilot would simply say an emotionless expletive. For Tom, the equivalent is "Oops."

I immediately looked down into the boat, because I figured the boat had sprung another leak and was sinking, but it was dry. Then I looked at Tom, who was looking at the supporting Bollman Steel Truss bridge pillars we were drifting under. Then I looked at the pillar that Tom was looking at. Then I read what Tom had just read. Then I mentally said "Oops." Painted on the pillar we were passing by was a white sign with red letters: "DANGER. DAM. 300 yards." People in the park simply watched as we became a flurry of activity. Tom dropped his camera gear, moved equipment away from the engine, flipped the starter switch, primed the carburetor, and pulled the crank. Nothing. We passed a sign pounded into the ground on the West Virginia shore: "DAM AHEAD. Boat Carry. W. Va. Side. 600 feet." Squeeze the fuel bulb again and pray

Tom didn't flood the engine. Pull the crank. Pull the crank. Pull the crank.

With a cough the engine idled up and Tom kicked it into gear. I braced myself for the wild 180-degree turn I thought he was going to make to get us back upstream to the park, but it didn't come. Tom wanted to get closer to the dam and the Potomac Edison power plant there along the shoreline. A barge with a crane on it was sitting in the river and had attracted Tom's attention. It appeared the crane was used to clear tree trunks and other debris away from the top of the dam and possibly repair parts of the dam. "Warning. Dam Ahead 100 yards." Now Tom swung the boat around and we headed back to the park.

We deflated the boat and put the boat and everything that was inside the boat back in the car. We then walked up the hill to find the cannon that was pictured in the Williamsport postcard I held in my hand. We couldn't figure out the angle in which the photograph was taken; surely the cannon wasn't sitting in the graveyard. It was. We found the cannon on top of the ridge in front of us—in River View Cemetery. There we found three cannon, and a worn-out sign that read:

Gen. Abner Doubleday

U.S.A.

Occupied This Site

1863

The story is that Abner Doubleday, a Union Army Major General, had a battery of artillerymen cross the Potomac River and throw up a breastwork so as to occupy this hill. Today it is either called "Doubleday Hill" or "Battery Hill." Officially it is the Doubleday Hill Monument which was erected in 1897. The monument overlooks the Potomac River into West Virginia and is maintained, with the cemetery, by the town of Williamsport. By the way, you may know that the Civil War began with the first Confederate cannon fired at Fort Sumter over Charleston Bay, South Carolina. You may be interested in knowing that the first Union shot returned from the fort was by the same Abner Doubleday who is buried in Arlington National Cemetery. And yes, this is the same Abner Doubleday who "invented" baseball, or rather, was the person who formalized the rules of the game by putting them in writing.

Behind the cemetery was the C&O Canal, which also could be seen from the hill. Tom and I were tired from our boat trip, which surprised us since we did very little but watch the scenery pass by and daydream. Before we left the town, we discovered that George Washington had met with the town founder, Otho Holland Williams. They met at the stone Spring House which once belonged to the Potomac traveler Thomas Cresap that is considered the oldest permanent building in Washington County. Their discussion, which also included another Williams (Colonel Elie Williams), on October 14, 1790, was to consider this small town of 'Williams Port' as the U.S. Capital. The result of that meeting was that the town was surveyed with extra-wide streets leading down to the Potomac to handle the expected mass of people and transportation. As we know, Williamsport lost to the marshy swamplands along the more navigable waters of the Potomac that is called the District of Columbia.

The next section of the Potomac we traveled down was from Williamsport to Shepherdstown, West Virginia. We parked near the Williamsport section of the C&O Canal just downstream from where we came ashore on our previous trip. To avoid the Potomac Edison dam, we carted the boat around the closed gate on the road leading into the Potomac Edison power plant, climbed off the road over a small hill and down to the river's edge. At the water, we looked upstream to see the small dam and some people fishing off the bank. Downstream we saw the Interstate 81 Bridge crossing the Potomac. We launched just upstream from a Williamsport sewer feeding into the river and soon found ourselves passing under the I-81 Bridge. Its five supporting columns kept the bridge high above the Potomac waters and our heads.

We passed under a railroad bridge and the very sad-looking remains of a bridge that probably collapsed during a major flood. All the other ruined bridges we had passed had their supporting columns intact with little damage. Only the top part of those passenger car or railroad bridges was missing. Here, much of the support beams were also missing and only clumps of the beams jutted vertically out of the river.

We made a turn to the right and had a straight shot of river for some two or three miles. Tom fired up the engine and took off, pleased that we could see what was ahead of us for so far. This would be the last time we had the luxury of seeing that far ahead before

reaching Shepherdstown. We passed a small island to our right and later passed an area called Cumberland Valley, where we then reached the next curve in the river. Tom killed the engine and we drifted around a curve in the river. We came across a very quiet and quaint town on our right called Falling Waters, West Virginia. Through the trees lining the West Virginia bank we could see areas of mowed grass and church spires rising toward the sky. If first impressions could be used to rate a town's personality, then this town would have received very high marks from us.

Then it was back to the reality of a river trying to find its way through the mountains. The chart showed that we had passed by the midpoint of the length of the C&O Canal. That brought little comfort to our thoughts of having to leave the end of the C&O Canal behind us in Georgetown and travel another roughly 150 miles to finish our trip. We reached the next curve in the river and this one was a sharp 90-degree turn to our left at a place called Opequon Junction, Maryland. We only recognized that from the charts we carried with us; we saw nothing but Opequon Creek flowing into the Potomac from the West Virginia side of the river. The Potomac curves were getting worse and they began to remind us of Paw Paw Bends. We would turn left at Opequon Junction, make another left and then make a wide swing to our right around Whiting's Neck, West Virginia. We noticed on the map that the C&O Canal disappears at this point. The towpath comes out to the river's edge. Years ago the canal barges would have had to come out into the river for about a mile before entering what was called the Inlet

Lock. That lock got them back into the canal. It wasn't that the canal had been completed at this point. It was just that the builders found it more useful to use the slack water of the Potomac at this point rather than wasting time to build a section of canal to hold the same slack water. The dozens of powerboats that were passing us, heading upstream and downstream, were getting on our nerves. Some were pulling skiers, a few were even sporting fishing poles but their lines were not in the water. Meanwhile, we could only see ahead of us a few hundred yards before the river would turn again. The reaction time of those driving powerboats to see us low in the water and avoid us was much less than the time we would have liked to have had. The loss of the C&O Canal and the mention of slack water reminded us that another dam, Feeder Dam Number 4, was fast approaching.

We passed Big Slackwater, Maryland, on our left and almost immediately pulled our boat ashore. We had further to walk and a further distance to drag the boat and gear this time than at Feeder Dam Number 5. We rested at the top of the viewing area for a few minutes where I read a sign about the dam. It said that Feeder Dam Number 4 was built between the years 1832 and 1834, which allowed slack water to form behind the dam. This slack water allowed boats to work their way upstream 15 miles to Williamsport with little difficulty. The winch house, located on the West Virginia side of the river, had been restored. We now understood why they used the actual Potomac rather than building a section of C&O Canal for the same purpose.

We walked our gear down past the dam and just past the two small islands downstream of the dam. When we saw two people fishing from a bassboat in the lee of the closer island, we disregarded the small eddies of whitewater still forming from the water coming over the dam. We decided to go ahead and drop the boat back into the water.

We reached another island where again we observed that all the tall trees were located on the downstream side of the island. We passed by the island, keeping it to our right, and soon afterward passed Taylor's Landing to our left. As the Potomac rounded Terrapin Neck with a right-hand turn, we caught a glimpse of some buildings on the Maryland side. This was the small town of Mercersville, named after the C&O Canal president, Charles Mercer. Little else kept our attention except that the river continued to flow first to the left and then to the right. We were on a constant watch for speeding boats and water skiers. Tom and I were just waiting for the time we would have to duck as a water skier's towline passed over us. We passed a boat ramp at Snyder's Landing, site of the Snyder coal and grain warehouse that was destroyed in the 1936 flood. Again we twisted with the river as it turned right, then left, then right again. Out of the corner of the bend we caught a glimpse of a bridge and congratulated ourselves on making it back to Shepherdstown, a small town boasting several "claims to fame." One is that it is the oldest inhabited community in West Virginia, founded by Thomas Shepherd in 1734. Another is that it is the site of the first successful steamboat. Another is that

Shepherdstown published the state's first newspaper in 1790. Both Shepherdstown and Williamsport, both small towns resting alongside the Potomac, have a quaint claim to fame to share. Shepherdstown and Williamsport (just 12 miles upstream on the Maryland side) each had the shot at becoming our Nation's Capital. After the Constitution was ratified and adopted, the long bitter debate began on the location of a Capital for the new United States. It had come down to debates between Alexander Hamilton and Thomas Jefferson. It was agreed that the Capital was to lie "at some place between the mouths of the Eastern Branch and the Conococheague." Well, the Eastern Branch of the Potomac is now better known as the Anacostia River and Williamsport is at the junction of the Potomac and Conococheague Creek. President George Washington was given the authority to choose the exact site between these two rivers.

We passed under the Route 34 Bridge, also called the James Rumsey Bridge. On a trip to Shepherdstown by car, we crossed over the same bridge. The James Rumsey Bridge was named in honor of the inventor who made successful public demonstrations of his steamboat on the Potomac River here on December 3rd and 11th, 1787.

The bridge itself was dedicated and opened to the public on July 15th, 1939. That suggested to us that the remains we were now passing by in our boat had probably been a working bridge until the 1936 flood.

Immediately passing the remains of that bridge, we pulled up onto an old boat ramp on the West Virginia side and made it back to our pre-staged car.

There was another reason we were here, and there was still some daylight left to find what we were looking for. We were looking for a tall granite column called the James Rumsey Monument near the West Virginia bank of the Potomac. The column was dedicated to the pioneer of steam-powered navigation and, like the sign said on the Rumsey Bridge. It is on these Potomac waters where he tested his inventions. As a point of trivia, James Rumsey also designed the C&O Canal locks at Great Falls. We found no signs leading to the column but we knew it was on the upstream side of the railroad bridge. Walking around one corner, we came across "No Trespassing" signs and a gate. The gate was built to swing open so that the end of the pole fit into a notch in another pole. It had not been opened in some time as seen by the honeysuckle vines that had been intertwining themselves around the gate. We slipped past the gate into a freshly mowed courtyard and saw ahead of us Rumsey's granite column rising some 100 feet into the air. At the column's apex was a globe and at its base was a plaque. The plaque read:

In honor of
JAMES RUMSEY
Inventor of the steamboat
Who in October, A.D. 1783, on the
Potomac River near the mouth
of Sir John's Run made the first
successful application of steam to
the practical purposes of navigation
and who on December 3rd, 1787, made
a further successful demonstration

on the Potomac River at Shepherdstown Virginia about three hundred
yards above this site.
Erected by
the State of West Virginia
under the auspices of
The Rumseyan Society
A.D. 1915

Unfortunately, James Rumsey died just four years after his tests and before he could exploit his successes. On the backside of the monument is another plaque that shows a relief of the steamboat. George Washington, in his diary of September 6th, 1784, wrote: "Saw boats made by James Rumsey for ascending currents by mechanics."

Then we noticed that a section of the monument grounds was roped off and a piece of the railing was missing. Upon closer inspection, it appeared that, except for mown grass, little else in the way of housekeeping was done to protect this monument from the normal wear and tear caused by Mother Nature and Father Time. The bushes and climbing vines were slowly covering the stone wall and a tree had fallen on the property. There were rival claims of John Fitch who claims to have done the same thing, and Robert Fulton's commercial success with the CLERMONT 20 years later, but Rumsey deserves the recognition and clearly gets it from looking at this monument.

Putting our boat back into the Potomac River, we continued our downstream journey. We floated past the remains of another bridge, past the James Rumsey Monument on our right, and then under a railroad bridge - all in just a few short minutes. Up ahead we saw another dam whose whitewater was enough for us to swing our boat over to the left bank and walk around. It is interesting that the "dam" that interrupted our journey downstream and forced us to walk around was the geological formation called Packhorse Ford. That crossing was considered the only good river crossing for many miles and before the bridges was built. Settlers who were moving south in the 1720s from as far north as York, Pennsylvania, followed an old Indian and packhorse trail that led them across the Potomac at this shallow. "Stonewall" Jackson crossed the Potomac at Packhorse Ford when he was travelling from Harpers Ferry to Sharpsburg. The Army of Northern Virginia crossed here after withdrawing from the bloody battles at Antietam.

It is said that at times the upper Potomac River ran so low during the dry season than it was easier for the Confederates to cross the Potomac than it was to cross the C&O Canal. It is a tribute to those who designed and built the canal. No one was able to blow up the locks or aqueducts of the canal, although they tried several times. You would need high explosives to succeed, and these were not easily available to the Confederates.

As we rounded the next bend, we came across a reluctant island called Knott Island. We called it reluctant because it was so close to the West Virginia shore we wondered if it really was an island at all during some summer dry spells. Directly across from the island was a C&O Canal aqueduct crossing Antietam Creek.

The Civil War was the event that spawned the birth of West Virginia. When the Civil War began, the state of Virginia extended along the entire length of the Potomac River and was bordered by the Chesapeake Bay and Atlantic Ocean on its eastern shore, to its northwest by the Ohio River and bordered by Kentucky, Ohio and Pennsylvania. The Civil War was the impetus needed for the western section of Virginia to pull away and become its own state. Since the Civil War was powerful enough to pit North against South and brother against brother, it was also powerful enough to rip Virginia in half. This war has its heroes and its monuments scattered all across the country, but no place can truly depict the horror of the Civil War like Antietam. Antietam Creek flows into the Potomac, and we stopped our journey down the river long enough to think about what had happened at Antietam so many years ago.

The Potomac played a major role in the Civil War. Soldiers fought on her with ships, walked through her in the shallower areas, crossed over her in portable pontoon bridges, and floated over her in balloons. The war affected all the towns along the river including Cumberland, Harpers Ferry, the District of Columbia, Quantico, and even Point Lookout, the Civil War prisoner-of-war camp. Today, sitting in a boat and staring under the C&O Canal aqueduct and up into Antietam Creek, I could barely put in words what is considered the bloodiest day on the Potomac.

Here Tom and I found us between the Blue Ridge and Allegheny Mountains in an area called the Great Appalachian Valley. It is one of the longest mountain valleys in the world and one of the most fertile regions in the United States. In Pennsylvania and Maryland it is known as the Cumberland Valley. In West Virginia and Virginia it is called the Shenandoah Valley.

Here, as in many miles of river now behind us, the Potomac is tranquil. The rolling hills make this a pastoral scene, yet all about you get the feeling that someone is talking to you but you just can't quite hear the voices. Later, at the Battlefield Site, I could still remember our conversation.

"Tom, I know this might sound strange, but do you feel something different about this place?" I asked, hoping halfway through that he had not heard the question. He was within earshot, but he didn't answer.

The noise is subconscious as your eyes beg to read the many bronze plaques and stone monuments rising up out of the landscape. It was at White's Ford near Leesburg, Virginia, from September 4 through 7, 1862, that General Robert E. Lee's Army of Northern Virginia splashed across the Potomac to invade the North. Major General George B. McClellan's Army of the Potomac set out to ensure that Lee would go no further.

While many in the past lost their lives to ravaging floods and Indian attacks on the Potomac, nothing could compare to the bloodiest battle of the Civil War - The Battle of Antietam. On September 17th, 1862, Lee threw his 55,000 men into battle against McClellan's 90,000 men. The reward if Lee had succeeded would have probably been a successfully negotiated peace based on Southern independence from the Union. McClellan's success would have probably meant the end of the Civil War. At the end of the day on September 17th, 23,000 Americans from both sides lay dead and dying on the Maryland battlefield. This was eight times more than were lost on the Normandy beaches on D-Day during World War II.

The battle was considered a draw. Neither side won any major victory, except that Lee's failure caused Great Britain to postpone official recognition of the Confederacy and gave President Abraham Lincoln the opportunity to issue the Emancipation Proclamation. Strategically, McClellan prevented Lee from moving further north and pushed him back south across the Potomac. With 23,000 Americans dead on the battlefields, neither side could really consider itself a winner. Shortly after the battle, President Lincoln removed McClellan from command. Lincoln stated that McClellan should have pursued Lee and his men across the Potomac because that would have probably ended the war right there. Some say that on September 17th, 1862, Antietam Creek ran red from all the blood flowing into it.

Antietam was originally built around a large iron works. The furnace started in 1765 by Joseph Chapline, the founder of Sharpsburg. The furnace closed in 1880 and little remains except for a kiln dated 1845. In its heyday, nine waterwheels operated the machinery, a forge with a 21-ton hammer, a rolling mill and a nail factory. A large number of cannon used in the Revolutionary War was cast here. Most of the machinery for Rumsey's steamboat was also made here.

As we stared at Antietam Creek pouring into the Potomac, three kayakers appeared on the creek, slipped under the aqueduct, paddled their way out into the Potomac and began heading downstream. The waters of the Potomac soon returned to that quiet river we had been enjoying these past few months. We pushed off from Knott Island to follow the kayakers.

Leaving Antietam Creek behind us, we watched the kayakers move over to the left and take the small dam that had appeared in front of them; we followed suit. A fishing boat was trolling just downstream from the dam and everyone in the boat had lines out. Houses appeared along the right-hand shore and piers and floating docks again appeared to sprout out from the West Virginia shoreline. A tall mountain appeared in front of us and the river obliged it by bending to the right and then back to the left to flow around it. More houses and piers appeared to our left. It looked like many had forgotten the high water levels on some previous floods and was determined to live close enough to get a good view of the Potomac.

Ever since leaving Antietam Creek we had been drifting away from it. Since leaving Antietam Creek, though, we never really drifted away from the impact that the Civil War played on this region. We were now approaching Harpers Ferry as few have, by boat on the Potomac than by boat on the C&O Canal.

Thomas Jefferson, after visiting Harpers Ferry in 1783, described his vivid impression of the natural setting.

"The passage of the Patowmac through the Blue Ridge is perhaps one of the most stupendous scenes in Nature." The impression continues:

"You stand on a very high point of land. On your right comes up the Shenandoah, having ranged along the foot of the mountains a hundred miles to seek a vent. On your left approaches the Potowmac in quest of a passage also. In the moment of their junction they rush together against the mountain, rend it asunder and pass off to the sea. The first glance of this scene hurries our senses into the opinion that the rivers began to flow afterwards, that in this place particularly they have been so dammed up by the Blue Ridge of mountains as to have formed an ocean which filled the whole valley; that, continuing to rise, down from its summit to its base. The piles of rock on each hand, but particularly on the Shenandoah, the evident marks of their disruptions and avulsions from their beds by the most powerful agents in nature has given the picture is of a very different character. It is a true contrast to the former. It is as placid and delightful as that is wild and tremendous. For the mountain being cloven asunder, she presents to your eye, through the cleft, a small catch of smooth blue horizon, at an infinite distance is that plain country, inviting you, as it were, from the riot and tumult roaring around to pass through the breach and participate in the calm below. Here the eye ultimately composes itself; and that way, too, the road happens actually to lead. You cross the Patowmac above the junction, pass along its side through the base of the mountains for three miles, the terrible precipice hanging in fragments above you, and within 20 miles reach Frederictown and the fine country around that. Yet here, as in the neighborhood of the Natural Bridge, are people who have passed their lives within a dozen miles and have never been to see these monuments of a war between rivers and mountains, which must have shaken the earth itself to its center."

The point from which Mr. Jefferson was inspired to write those words is called Jefferson Rock.

In 1761, the Virginia General Assembly granted Robert Harper the right to establish and maintain a ferry across the Potomac River. Harper had been providing ferry service since 1747, and Peter Stephens before operated a small ferry. Now a ferry concession had been awarded, giving Harper exclusive rights to transport foot and wagon traffic across the Potomac River at a place now called Harpers Ferry. Before that the area was called "The Hole." In colonial days "hole" meant a milieu or vicinity, however, it could also have something to do with the two converging rivers eating away at the mountains and producing a sheer rock cliff on one side. Tom and I had visited Harpers Ferry even before we started the book. We walked the streets, climbed to the top of the hill where Jefferson wrote those inspirational words, crossed the river into Maryland, and played tourist. While we were taking photographs of the confluence of the Potomac and the Shenandoah rivers, the idea of the book unknowingly formed as we toured the site and watched the rivers merge and move downstream.

It was during the Civil War that abolitionist John Brown from Kansas tried to start an uprising of the black slaves by locking himself with others inside the arsenal at Harpers Ferry. Others barricaded themselves in another house along the Potomac riverbank. Thirty-two hours later, U.S. Marines commanded by then Colonel Robert E. Lee stormed the buildings and captured Brown. John Brown was hanged for treason, but not before getting the last word in and accurately predicting the Civil War.

If you thought that the Civil War was harsh on the town of Harpers Ferry, what Mother Nature has done to the town is even worse. Harpers Ferry is the lowest point of land in West Virginia and has suffered grievously from a succession of floods. The town and the surrounding areas reflect a war-torn atmosphere of abandoned bridge supports and high water marks.

Robert Harper noted the first recorded flood in February 1748, followed by the "Pumpkin" flood of 1753. The "Pumpkin" flood occurred in the fall of 1753 after the pumpkins had been harvested and stored in winter supply huts along the river. The flood washed thousands of pumpkins downstream making for an interesting sight. The catastrophic changes in the forests wrought by the early settlers are reflected in the severity of the floods. As the region along the Potomac was settled further and further upstream, the area of forestland and the numbers of trees and shrubs declined drastically. The settlers began cutting down and burning trees to fuel furnaces of developing industries. The farmers also cleared the land of trees so that they could plow and raise crops. For years nothing

stronger than grasses and weeds grew in the upper Potomac region. As settlers continued to chop down trees and turned forests into farmland, the ability of the land to retain water was reduced. The floods with their destructive power increased in intensity. Henry Lee, who was granted land now called Sully near Dulles Airport, wrote in 1732 that he was happy to see brush fires built by freeholders to remove the unwanted trees and shrubs. The Great Falls area, for example, was farmed extensively for about 120 years, but gradually, as the cultivated fields were abandoned, forest plants again started to grow. Fast-growing pines were at first dominant but hardwoods slowly made their comeback, and the severity of the floods decreased.

The 1810 flood was hailed as a record breaker. Although little is known about the flood, it was the first of a series of fatal floods that would strike for the rest of the century. Three record floods were recorded during 1843. The April flood crested a foot higher than the 1810 flood and ruined the early planting. The mid-September flood caused more damage, including wiping out the gardens ready for harvest that had been replanted after the April flood. A late-September flood crested three feet higher than the April 1810 flood, completely ruining the year's harvest. Still, these floods were of little consequence when compared to the 1852 flood.

The 1852 flood rose at least six feet higher than any previous flood. It began as a gentle rain but after three solid days of rain, the Potomac could no longer hold it all. Nearly every building along the streets closest to the river was destroyed, and all bridges except the Winchester Railroad Bridge were toppled. Yet even the 1852 flood was just a warning to the greater floods that would come later.

Harpers Ferry lies at the confluence of the Potomac and Shenandoah Rivers. These two rivers together drain the water off some 10,000 square miles of land at an average annual precipitation of 40 inches. All this water meets at Harpers Ferry and flows through "The Gap" in the Blue Ridge Mountains to continue down the Potomac.

Another flood came in 1859, another in 1860, and another in 1861. Floods had become so commonplace that a newspaper account of one flood stated that "all the basements of the houses on Shenandoah Street, Harpers Ferry, were, of course, flooded." When the 1870 flood, many Harpers Ferry residents thought it would just be another flood. Historians now call the 1870 flood the greatest natural disaster ever to befall that town. Homes were swept away in the middle of the night. One newspaper correspondent wrote about the dying wails of friends that could be heard throughout the night as the river turned into one angry sea of rolling waves and swept them and their homes downstream.

In May 1889, the same weather system that destroyed Johnstown, Pennsylvania, and killed over 2,000 Johnstown residents, also raised the Potomac and Shenandoah Rivers seven feet higher than any previously recorded flood at Harpers Ferry. At one time the floodwaters rose one foot in 15 minutes. Nearly every bridge upstream, around Harpers Ferry

and downstream to Weverton and Point of Rocks were destroyed. One that survived, the Baltimore & Ohio Railroad Bridge at Harpers Ferry, did so by weighing the bridge down with loaded coal hoppers from one end of the bridge to the other. One report stated: "The waves of the Potomac were seen to lash themselves into fury over the rocky bed below the bridges. Further on the river rolled in a resistless torrent until it was lost to view a mile or two below by a bend to the right." The C&O Canal was damaged so severely that it took some time to place it back into operation again. The Spring 1924 flood did so much damage to the C&O Canal at Harpers Ferry that it did not open for the 1924 shipping season - or ever again. The 1924 flood sounded the death knell for industry in Harpers Ferry. Those industries that survived the Civil War still relied on water to power their plants - and the dams, raceways and floodgates they used were swept away during the 1924 flood and never replaced. Heavy industry simply gave up and moved out of the area.

The March 1936 flood broke every previous flood record on the books for the Harpers Ferry area and is considered the granddaddy of all floods to have swept down the Potomac. The 1936 flood crested at 36.5 feet.

One Potomac flood occurred during World War II and was considered so devastating that information about the damage caused by the flood was classified to prevent our enemies from finding out about our loss of communications and roads. The flood occurred in October 1942 and a 17.5-inch rainfall was recorded upstream from Harpers Ferry at Riverton, while

Harpers Ferry itself recorded 6.5 inches. Later, 7.25 inches of rainfall would be recorded at Harpers Ferry in 1972, brought in by the remnants of Hurricane Agnes. It was enough water to see the Potomac crest at over 30 feet above flood stage.

Another flood was the Valentine's Day Flood in February 1984. One newspaper reported that floodwaters just below Williamsport had forced the removal of house trailers from the Potomac Fish and Game Club. Not all were removed in time.

The Washington Post newspaper characterized the 1985 flood as one of "unprecedented destruction." Paw Paw was flooded as nearly 18 inches of rain fell in the upper Potomac region. The raging Potomac crested at 54 feet above flood stage at Paw Paw and easily took out the Paw Paw Bridge. Residents were forced to drive 25 miles for food and gasoline. Although Harpers Ferry received less than 2 inches of rain, the floodwaters from upstream were heading down toward the town. When the floodwaters hit Harpers Ferry they were travelling at over 20 miles an hour. A person can barely stand in three feet of water moving at 2 miles an hour. I remember standing on the Francis Scott Key Bridge that connects Rosslyn, Virginia, with Georgetown in the District of Columbia and watching the large trees, dead animals and floating debris floating downstream. One humorous mention was the Volkswagen Beetle that was seen floating downstream. Watermark stains can still be seen on the boathouses that line the Georgetown shore. For now, though, we had the pleasure of being nowhere near the ravages of those floodwaters.

As we came around a left bend in the river we were met with whitewater as far as we could see downstream. That was enough wild water for us. We pulled the boat out of the water on the Maryland side at Feeder Dam Number 3. This dam was built in 1799 and, after being damaged in the 1810 flood, was rebuilt in 1820. Like the other dams built for the C&O Canal, this one allowed the passage of Potomac water into the canal through an inlet lock. Walking around the feeder dam, we cautiously put the boat back in the water and hugged the left bank as we continued down this area that is called The Needles. We were approaching Harpers Ferry. To our left were the sheer cliffs of the Blue Ridge Mountains and to our right was the somewhat flat expanse from which Harpers Ferry was born. It took the combined efforts of the Potomac and Shenandoah rivers and many years to downcut their way through the Blue Ridge Mountains here at Harpers Ferry.

Charles Thomas, secretary of the Continental Congress and friend of Thomas Jefferson, visited Harpers Ferry and spoke of the place in one long rambling sentence:

> "The reflections I was led into on viewing this passage of the Patowmac through the Blue ridge were, that this country must have suffered some violent convulsion, and that the face of it must have been changed from what it probably was some centuries ago: that the broken and ragged rocks, which are left with one end fixed in the precipice, and the other jutting out, and seemingly ready to fall

for want of support; the bed of the river for several miles below obstructed, and filled with loose stones carried from this mound; in short, every thing on which you cast your eye evidently demonstrates a disrupture and breach in the mountain, and that, before this happened, what is now a fruitful vale, was formerly a great lake or collection of water, which possibly might have formed a mighty cascade, or had its vent to the ocean by the Susquehanna, where the Blue ridge seems to terminate."

On a more subdued Potomac, we drifted under the railroad bridges and onto a sandy beach at the top of the T, where we came ashore. In front of us the Potomac made a sharp 90-degree turn to the left while the Shenandoah River passed us from right to left along the top of the T. We packed up our belongings, climbed to the level of the C&O Canal, then climbed the stairs and crossed the Potomac using the separated passenger side of the railroad bridge. We were walking out of Maryland, walking into West Virginia and seeing Virginia to our left across the Shenandoah River. For the brief time that we spent crossing the railroad bridge, we were on what many feel should be a part of the Appalachian Trail instead of the Route 340 Bridge. The Appalachian Trail is considered the longest footpath in the world. It stretches 2,049 miles from Mount Katadin in Maine to Mount Oglethorpe in Georgia, and crosses the Potomac only once at Harpers Ferry. The trail was built between 1922

and 1937 by volunteers and is maintained today by volunteer clubs such as the Appalachian Trail Club.

We walked through town and to our car. We returned often to Harpers Ferry and it is one of our favorite spots along the Potomac. We would watch the trains cross the bridge over the river and disappear into the tunnel on the Maryland side. We would also watch people floating on inflated inner tubes drift past Harpers Ferry on the Shenandoah River, visit many shops in town and climb up to Jefferson Rock to view the area as Thomas Jefferson once did.

CHAPTER 3

From Harpers Ferry, West Virginia, to Great Falls and the American Legion Bridge

We wisely agreed to bypass the next mile of Potomac water below the confluence of the Potomac and the Shenandoah Rivers. This mile of river is called White Horse Rapids and it is a passage taken only by the most experienced whitewater boaters. We walked along the Maryland side and crossed a bridge over the railroad tracks that were partly torn out. Down the bank we could see whitewater. We were generalists, getting to know a little of everything there was to know concerning the river. We were not yet specialists at maneuvering through Potomac whitewater. We remembered the Kitzmiller area and the surprise waterfall at Cumberland, so we were more than happy to watch from shore. The kayakers fought the water, bounced off rocks and sometimes lost their kayaks out from under them. We even saw one kayaker give up trying to right himself after being flipped over. He pulled himself out of the kayak while underwater, and then hung onto the water-filled kayak as he tried to swim out of the main current of the river. He eventually succeeded with the help of another kayaker. It was enough of a spectacle to make us feel we had made the right choice in walking this portion of the river. We walked along the C&O Canal path, which is also part of the Appalachian Trail for almost two miles. As we walked we caught glimpses of the river and kayakers.

We walked past Canal Lock 31 and then between the ridges of South Mountain. This mountain ridge, like the Blue Ridge, had also been eroded by thousands of years of Potomac waters flowing past. We traveled by foot as far as Mountain Road at a place called Hobo Jungle. With many sidetracks of the Baltimore and Ohio (B&O) railroad located here and the somewhat uninhabited and quiet area, Hobo Jungle was a popular hobo gathering spots in the area and was most famous in the 1920s and 1930s.

We noticed that all the kayakers were pulling their kayaks out of the water at Mountain Road. We overheard some of them talking about encountering swift water at Short Hill Rapid and at Knoxville Rapid. These were calm waters today.

We put our boat into the water after Mountain Road and floated quietly down a shallow path of water for nearly a half-mile. We then reentered the main body of the Potomac.

The Potomac immediately widened to about 250 feet and became shallow - we had entered the flood plains of the river. We wondered how this area would look while carrying the melting snows of Spring from upstream. We figured the small islands we were looking at would disappear underwater and that it would not be nearly as safe as in the middle of summer. Another bridge appeared before us and our waterproof chart showed this to be the Brunswick Bridge at Brunswick, Maryland. Marylanders call the road crossing the bridge "Route 17;" Virginians call it "Route 267." In either case, we drifted silently under it, passed two small islands that the chart showed as one, apparently due to erosion. Brunswick was laid out in 1780 by Leonard Smith and was originally called Barry Post Office and later, Berlin. The railroad changed the name to Brunswick in 1890, as there was already another Berlin, Maryland.

We were on a slow boat to Washington at this point as we barely felt ourselves moving along. Matching our position against the shoreline as we passed the Brunswick Municipal Park, we noticed that we were probably travelling slower than had we walked this area. We came to a bend in the Potomac that ran C&O Canal. Rounding the bend, we began passing several small islands. One was Bald Eagle Island, but there were so many small islands we couldn't figure out which one was Bald Eagle Island. We didn't we see any bald eagles or even their nests. The islands then began to get larger as we passed them in succession.

Crossing the Potomac — General Jubal Early Car and Passenger Ferryboat

us to our right, but we pushed ourselves left as we rounded the bend. Looking up Catoctin Creek on the Maryland side, we saw the Catoctin Aqueduct of the We stayed to the left of the islands and missed seeing the other Catoctin creek flowing into the Potomac from the Virginia side. The Catoctin Creek flowing into the

Potomac from the Maryland side and the Catoctin Creek flowing in from the Virginia side are only similar in name. The water flowing from the creek on the Maryland side is clear while the water from Virginia is usually yellow and muddy from mineral deposits and pollution flowing down the creek. We drifted by, trying to convince ourselves that the extra water flowing out of these two creeks had sped up our downstream journey. Before we could take any shoreline measurements we had drifted between the ridges of the Catoctin Mountains and reached Point of Rocks, Maryland. The Route 15 Bridge passed high above our heads. The arguments between the builders of the C&O Canal and the Baltimore and Ohio Railroad hit their climax over Point of Rocks. Geographically, there is only a narrow ledge through the Catoctin Mountains along the Potomac just wide enough for either railroad tracks or a canal, but not both. The court favored the canal and the B&O Railroad had to dig a tunnel through the mountains at Point of Rocks. George Snouffer built the first house at Point of Rocks in the early 1700s. The rock point for which the town the named was destroyed during the building of the present road bridge now crossing the Potomac at Point of Rocks.

We continued our downstream run, convinced we would make it to Algonkian Park before dark. The scenery was beautiful, though, which made the time go a little faster, although the Potomac was not cooperating with much of a current. After passing under the bridge the Potomac forked around Heaters Island, a state wildlife management area, and we took the left fork. Heater's Island was settled by Conooi Indians in 1699 and was called Conoy Island in 1711. The Conooi Indians resided here when they had to abandon their lands in Charles County. Here they built a large fort with about 18 structures inside the fort and nine outside. A smallpox epidemic hit the island in 1705, killing all the inhabitants.

We drifted past an area called Calico Rocks, Maryland. "Calico Rock" is multi-colored limestone that is also affectionately known as Potomac Marble. Those living in the Washington, D.C., area can see this type of limestone—it was used in the construction of the U.S. Capitol building.

We were still in the flood plains and this area got our nomination for the flattest part of the Potomac above Great Falls. Below Great Falls the Potomac is on the Coastal Plain and is influenced by the tides because it is at sea level. Now we were on the Piedmont portion of the Potomac. While the volume of water had dramatically increased, we were expecting a stronger current but found that as the river widened the current remained pretty much the same —nice and slow. We floated past high hills on the Maryland side and smaller, but still high, bluffs on the Virginia side. What the river had done by eroding the hills was to produce a pleasant and beautiful valley. We passed Mason Island and Nolands Island.

Noland not only had an island in the Potomac but also ran a ferry. The ferry was at a place along the Potomac considered by historians to be one of the oldest crossing places along the river. It was discovered to be the "Warrior Path" of the Catoctin Indians. A ferry had been operating here since as far back as 1758 and Nolands Ferry was the scene of several Civil War Potomac River crossings. After passing several other islands, the river made a 90-degree bend to the right where it became a geographic repeat of what we saw back at Catoctin Creek. This time, though, we watched the Monocacy River flow south into the Potomac and the C&O Canal's Monocacy Aqueduct cross over the Monocacy River. This aqueduct was huge. The Monocacy Aqueduct was completed in 1833, and railroad tracks had to be laid for five miles to transport stone from a quarry to the aqueduct site. This aqueduct is one of the canal's most outstanding structures.

Tom had enough drifting for awhile, so he pumped the primer ball on the hose leading from the gas tank to the outboard motor, cranked over the engine and got us moving a bit faster downstream. We passed a Potomac Electric Power Company (PEPCO) power plant on our left and past a shallow area called White's Ford. It was at White's Ford where General Robert E. Lee crossed the Potomac on his way to Antietam. General Jubal Early also used it after his raid on Washington in 1864. We came down to another fork and took the right one this time, as it was the larger of the two passages. We were passing Lower Mason Island to our left and had nearly forgotten that there was another part of the Potomac River behind the island until, nearly two miles later, the other part of the Potomac reemerged to join us. We passed Limestone Branch Creek on our right and just ahead, the 1954-built "General Jubal Early" ferry

at White's Ferry was transporting cars from Virginia into Maryland. Once there were some 100 ferries in use crossing the Potomac. Today, only one continues operation.

On a previous occasion, we decided that there was still enough daylight to enjoy a ferryboat trip across the Potomac at White's Ferry near Poolesville in Montgomery County, Maryland. The first house erected in the area was in 1793 by John Poole. It is still standing on Fisher Avenue in spite of the three major fires that have ravaged the town. The ferry at Poolesville happens to be one of the few fresh water, captive (cable-guided) ferry left in operation in the United States. There used to be many more, most notably Nolands Ferry whose site we passed about 10 miles back, and Edward's Ferry whose site was still 10 miles ahead. As we drove up to the river's edge by car, a sign greeted us:

GEN JUBAL A. EARLY
Whites Ferry, Maryland.
Open 6 a.m. Closed 11 p.m.
Flash lights or
blow horn for ferry.

Land records for the area show that ferries had been operating from this general area since 1833. The one in use today is the General Jubal A. Early that was built in Baltimore. The last time White's Ferry stopped making trips across the river, if you don't include Mother Nature, was during World War II. It began work again in 1954 and has been doing so ever since. Little did we realize that we were continuing the tradition of ferry crossings made very important during the Civil War.

During the early stages of the Civil War, there were many places to cross the Potomac in this area, including permanent bridges. On June 9th, 1861, Colonel Thomas J. Jackson (who earned the nickname "Stonewall" a month later at Bull Run) ordered all the bridges burned. This made the ferries all that more important. A Civil War battle took place here around White's Ferry, and the ferry even had something to do with it. The battle became known as the Battle of Balls Bluff.

On October 20th, 1861, General Stone, the Union commander occupying the area in Maryland around White's Ferry (then called Conrad's Ferry) was ordered by General McClellan to send a reconnaissance patrol across the river. The patrol was to head toward Leesburg to see if there was time to keep Leesburg from falling into Confederate hands. General Stone decided to send more than one reconnaissance patrol just in case and sent one unit to wade across the Potomac via Harrison's Island on October 20, 1861. He then sent another unit to cross the Potomac at White's Ferry. On the 21st of October he sent some 2,500 men from the 1st Minnesota Regiment and the 82nd New York Regiment across the river at Edward's Ferry. Once the Union soldiers had crossed the Potomac, the Confederates came out of hiding and the Union soldiers never got any closer to Leesburg than the Virginia bank of the Potomac. The Battle of Balls Bluff had begun. Forced off the bluff by the Confederates, the Union soldiers found themselves pinned down

in Confederate crossfire with the Potomac flowing between them and their safety. The boats that were used to carry them across were destroyed or set free to drift downstream, and the Union soldiers then had a choice to make - to be killed there along the shoreline, or swim for it. About 50 Union soldiers died along the shore that day, but more than 700 were missing by the end of the battle, many killed in the panic swim back across the Potomac, their bodies floating downstream.

Of the more than 150 Union soldiers wounded that day was the then Lieutenant Oliver Wendell Holmes, who later went on to become a Supreme Court Justice.

The graves of many of the 50 Union soldiers who died along the banks of the Potomac now rest in the smallest National Cemetery in the United States - at Balls Bluff overlooking White's Ferry.

The ferry played a part in a daring and, as the war progressed, one of the more desperate campaigns of the war. In June 1864, Union General Ulysses S. Grant was threatening the Confederates in Richmond and Petersburg, Virginia. Confederate General Robert E. Lee than sent General Jubal A. Early up the Shenandoah Valley to attack Maryland. This drew some of Grant's troops away from the action taking place further south. Early crossed the Potomac and entered Maryland, and after a few attention-drawing victories, had found himself within sight of Washington, just as Lee had planned. General Grant then obliged Lee by sending Union troops north to chase General Early back into Virginia, which he did at Edward's Ferry on June 13, 1864.

The ferry's cable stretches across the width of the river and is attached to the side of the ferry. A large motor on the ferry turns the wheels that the cable is attached to and pulls the ferry across the river. We passed over the cable and again the river forked and we floated left down the larger of the two forks. We found ourselves passing Harrison Island - the largest island along the entire Potomac River. Two miles later the two forks of the Potomac rejoined.

The slowness of the river gave Tom and I time to discuss how we were going to handle the most dangerous part of the Potomac, Great Falls, which we were slowly drifting toward. Like a black hole in space or a huge vortex, we were sucked toward Great Falls. The thought of being swept into Great Falls and becoming a statistic was disconcerting. We passed Maryland's Broad Run on our left, rounded a slight bend in the Potomac to our right, and came across two interesting points along the river.

The first sight was Edwards Ferry along the Maryland shore and now identified by the lone boat ramp. Edwards Ferry was the site of another major Civil War crossing. This time the Federal Army of the Potomac heading toward Gettysburg in June 1863 did the crossing. The ferry operated here until 1936. The second interesting sight was directly across from Edwards Ferry at Goose Creek, Virginia. We already know something about the C&O Canal. Later we'll talk some about George Washington's Pawtomack Canal and even the Alexandria Canal that ran from present-day Key Bridge at Georgetown in Washington, D.C., to Old Town, Virginia. One of the least known sets of canals and locks along the Potomac is along Goose Creek. The plan was to build a 20-mile system of canals and locks to provide transportation for Virginia farmers needing to transport their goods downstream. Once the goods had made it to the Potomac, they would have to cross the Potomac and enter the Goose Creek River Lock on the C&O Canal. From there they followed the C&O Canal downstream to Georgetown. Work began in 1849, but only 12 miles were completed. When Tom and I were there the locks and canals were sitting on property owned by the Xerox Corporation, home of the nearby Xerox International Center for Training and Management Development Facility. While there was talk some years ago by Xerox to restore all or part of the Goose Creek canal and lock system, nothing has yet been done. The Training Center is today called the National Conference Center in the newly created area called Lansdowne.

We passed Cabin Branch flowing into the Potomac on our left and then passed Selden Island on our right. At the downstream side of Selden Island, it appeared that a smaller chunk of the island had separated from the main island. So much had broken off that the smaller part was given its own name - Van Deventer Island. Behind these islands, Virginia's Broad Run was flowing into the Potomac. On our left we passed Sycamore Landing. A repeat of an island breaking apart occurred at the downstream tip of Van Deventer Island. This was on a much smaller scale, but not too small to miss giving this new island another name. This time we floated past Tenfoot

Island. Tenfoot Island has a major "claim-to-fame" as the home to one of the largest moonshine stills to operate in the Washington area during Prohibition. The moonshiners even built concrete ramps on both sides of the island to allow for the unloading of raw materials and the loading of their distilled products. While everyone knew what was going on, the stills were never raided.

Directly past this island we looked to our right and saw a boat ramp on the property of the Algonkian Regional Park. We slipped between Tenfoot Island and Sharpshin Island and continued floating downstream on the right-hand side of the river. We passed Sugarland Run pouring into the Potomac and then entered a large flatwater section created by the backup of water behind the old C&O canal dam at the start of the Seneca rapids.

This area on the Potomac is called affectionately Seneca Lake and we watched carefully as motorboats pulled water-skiers through the water. One came close to us, and there really isn't that much maneuvering room. The same Rules of the Road apply here on the Potomac as they apply on the Chesapeake Bay or on the ocean—boats without motors running have the right-of-way over boats using their motors.

With the backup of water, there was little current, but it was enough for us to realize that we needed the engine to push us over to Seneca Creek. With our own engine noise mixed in with the noise of other motorboats, we headed for the Maryland shore. The C&O Canal Seneca Aqueduct is the most unique aqueduct we passed. At this confluence of Seneca

Creek and the Potomac River lie the remains of the collapsed Seneca Aqueduct. It remains stable enough for hikers to cross the aqueduct and hike upstream to see the old skirting basin built for the Patowmack Canal. This canal bridge over Seneca Creek was a combination of a lock and an aqueduct. Since the land was too low here, the aqueduct passing over Seneca Creek had to be built higher than normal. This allows for passage under the aqueduct for those using the creek. To build the aqueduct high enough to allow passage beneath it, the builders had to bring the water level up higher along the canal for the barges to pass across the aqueduct. Using a lock at the aqueduct did this. The hikers were heading toward a basin which once allowed canal boats a safer downstream trip than taking the main Potomac across the Seneca Breaks. The area has now become largely a swamp only of great interest to birdwatchers. This area also provides access to a view of the remains of the old Seneca Sandstone Quarry and Stone-Cutting Mill. This mill was stone cutting mill, and the red sandstone used for the original Smithsonian "Castle" on the Mall was quarried here. The mill also provided its red sandstone for the Cabin John Bridge.

It was time for us to pull the boat and gear out of the water. What lay ahead was Rowser's Ford, Feeder Dam Number 2, and the Seneca Rapids. General J.E.B. Stuart used Rowser's Ford as a crossing point during the Civil War on June 27th, 1863. This was done to enter Maryland from Virginia on his ride around the Union Army during the Gettysburg Campaign. Feeder Dam Number 2 is made of stone rubble and stretches across the entire width of the Potomac: 2,500 feet. The dam was used to siphon water off the Potomac and pour it into the C&O Canal.

We were warned about Seneca Rapids by kayakers standing around in a local outdoor camping supply store. They said that it starts out simple enough, with small riffles at the backwater beckoning you on. It gets tricky to maneuver when you cross the remains of the old C&O canal feeder dam. They agreed that we would be tossed around trying to avoid the ledges, only to find out that we also needed to avoid the rocks that have been pushed up into small piles by the current. We didn't see any kayakers on this stretch of the river. We did see how they would have to squeeze between narrow passages of water that would be moving faster than the kayak. On the Potomac, where we drifted at various speeds according to where we were on the river, we were constantly readjusting our thinking. Not reacting correctly meant we found ourselves turned sideways on the river, and in a position that could upset the boat and flip us over, with all our gear. When we found ourselves turned sideways, the rudder no longer worked, and we had to use our oars to straighten out. We decided to walk the Seneca Rapids portion of the Potomac from the safety of the towpath along the C&O Canal.

We walked downstream past Seneca Creek for a mile when we passed Pond Island and saw that the river was beginning to shrink. We had reached Blockhouse Point; an undeveloped forested tract called Blockhouse Point Park administered by the Maryland-National Capital Park and Planning Commission; and

the beginning of the Dierssen Waterfowl Sanctuary. The bluffs along Blockhouse Point reach a height of 125 feet and provided us with a scenic view of the river, Seneca Rapids, and Seneca Dam. Across from Blockhouse Point, hugging the Virginia shoreline, we saw Elm Island. As we continued our walk past the Seneca Rapids we reached Watkins Island one half mile later, and saw Muddy Branch feeding its waters into the Potomac. We decided this was where we would continue our trip from the water. We noticed the C&O Canal's Lock No. 22, known as Pennyfield Lock. This is the premier site for Potomac-bound birdwatchers and one of the most scenic sections along the C&O Canal towpath.

Later we traveled by car down Seneca Road on the Virginia side of the rapids to view the remains of the old canal once belonging to George Washington's Potowmack Canal Company. While on the Virginia side, we walked past Patowmack Island and Elm Island until we could see where we were going to drop the boat back in the water.

We returned to the Maryland side by driving down Pennyfield Lock Road. We inflated our boat that went into Muddy Branch, and we paddled our way back out into the river. Watkins Island was directly in front of us when we entered the Potomac. Other large and small islands passed us as we drifted by, the sound of many birds emanating from the trees. We were taking it slow at this point, peering at things along the riverbank through our cameras' zoom lenses, munching on snacks. Then the thought crossed my mind that this was going to be one our shortest trips on the river.

"Aren't we getting close to Great Falls?" Tom asked.

I pulled out the notes I had made months ago especially for this trip and saw in big red letters: DO NOT miss the takeout at the Maryland Great Falls Park; DO NOT try for the Virginia side; DO NOT attempt the low dam upstream from the falls; DO NOT be lured by the fast water along the left shore; Watch for the warning buoys; Stay Alert or Become a Statistic. I had an instant overload of information coming at me.

"Tom," I said a bit anxiously, "I have never read anything written about Great Falls from a person who had gone over the falls in a boat. You want to make sure we hit the shoreline in plenty of time?"

"No problem," Tom replied. "Besides, we haven't even made it around the bend ... Hey, do you hear that noise? I think we're too close!"

My heart stopped for a split second until I saw Tom's face and realized he was pulling my leg. I tried to shrug it off. When we passed Gladys Island at the downstream tip of Watkins Island, I had changed the subject and was now talking about gold. This region is pockmarked with hundreds of caves and trenches dug by people suffering from gold fever. Over the past 100 years or so, more than 5,000 ounces of gold have been mined out of the Maryland earth, with many mines located in this area along the Potomac. Some mines still exist and are boarded up to prevent people from entering the weakened tunnels; still, the boards

are removed sometimes by either gold fever sufferers or teenagers looking for thrills. The most systematic search for gold along the Potomac began in 1915 when a mining geologist by the name of A. A. Hassan directed an exploration that included 12 miles of open trenches scattered over 1,200 acres. The trenches are still visible. Near the intersection of Falls Road and MacArthur Boulevard is the Maryland Mine. This mine, according to a legend probably created by the National Park Service to keep people away, is haunted.

Gold was first discovered in the area in 1714 by German miners at the headwaters of Potomac Creek, Virginia, a few miles downstream from where we were now. An 1834 report noted that "many bags of gold shipped from Aquila Wharf." Along the upper Potomac, though, a 1951 U.S. Bureau of Mines report states that the upper Potomac mines had a production of 6,102 ounces before being closed. People can still be seen today along the creeks flowing into the Potomac panning for those minute flecks of gold.

We passed Beall Island to the left of us and began seeing dozens of aluminum flat-bottomed boats. They all looked the same and were painted the same color. Only when we came out from behind a stand of smaller islands did we recognize what was going on. The National Park Service rented out these boats at Virginia's Riverbend State Park.

I knew we were closing in on Great Falls because Riverbend Park is several hundred acres of mostly undeveloped land along the Potomac just upstream from Great Falls on the Virginia side. Administered by the Fairfax County Park Authority, it has visitors' center adjoining picnic grounds and a boat livery, nature trails and a few unmarked hiking trails. The Riverbend area differs from Great Falls in that there are fewer rocks in the river and along the shore. It is typical flat Piedmont country and we have since gone back to this park with our wives for some enjoyable afternoon picnics.

I made sure Tom was swinging the boat over to the left and hugging the Maryland shore as we passed Conn Island. We poked our way downstream, breaking away from the shoreline long enough to go around the trees that were sticking out over the bank. These trees looked like they were ready to drop into the river during the next flood. Tom then saw a flat spot on the shore and swung the boat up onto the bank.

After cleaning up, we walked back to the overlook platform that looks out over the aqueduct dam and water supply intakes. The Potomac River just above Great Falls has been the principal source of water for the Washington and surrounding cities for more than 150 years. The dam was built in the 1850s and the structure is 2,877 feet long and between 10 to 15 feet high. The dam diverts about 200 million gallons of water a day into the intakes on the Maryland side. The water travels down through aqueducts to the District of Columbia, Arlington, and Falls Church, Virginia. The U.S. Army Corps of Engineers operates the entire aqueduct system. The aqueduct system carries the diverted waters about 10 miles downstream to the Dalecarlia Water Treatment Plant. A unique feature of the aqueduct system is the Cabin John Bridge that is discussed in the next chapter.

For now, we would hike beside the 15 miles of falls and rapids and view the rushing waters from the banks of both the Maryland and Virginia sides.

Great Falls Park is an 800-acre area between the water supply dam above Great Falls and Difficult Run. The National Park Service manages it. It is here where one can view the Potomac dropping a total of 60 feet from the Great Falls Dam to the base of the falls. Tom and I were not the first ones to be enthralled by the Potomac and especially the Great Falls area. Thomas Jefferson, during his long and productive life, wrote and published only one full-length book: "Notes on the State of Virginia," first published in 1787. In that book, he described the Potomac River that is used as a state boundary dividing portions of West Virginia, Virginia, Maryland and Washington, D.C., from each other. A fathom, by the way, is six feet.

The Patowmac is 7 1/2 miles wide at the mouth; 4-1/2 at Nomony bay; 3 at Aquia; 1-1/2 at Hallooing point; 1-1/4 at Alexandria. Its soundings are, 7 fathom at the mouth; 5 at St. George's island; 4-1/2 at Lower Matchodic; 3 at Swan's point, and thence up to Alexandria. These falls are 15 miles in length, and of very great descent, and the navigation above them for bateaux and canoes, is so much interrupted as to be little used.

I look forward for the times I could spring a little more trivia on Tom, and today was one of those times. As we stood on the platform overlooking the falls, I nonchalantly said, "Tom, what is the second largest falls in the United States in terms of volume of water?"

"Okay," Tom said, smiling. "Everyone knows that Niagara Falls is the largest, so considering where we're standing, the answer is probably Great Falls."

In terms of volume of water, the Potomac has been flowing through this area for the past 180 million years or so. It is here at Great Falls where the most spectacular landscape features of the length of the river can be seen. Great Falls is richer in scenery, history and nature than possibly anywhere else along the river. It has influenced the lives and fortunes of those that

have lived in the Potomac Valley for centuries, and countless generations of Indians used it as a place to gather, to trade, and to fish. For the early settlers it was also a barrier to river navigation, an obstacle that canal builders on both sides of the Potomac struggled to overcome.

The Potomac that we had come to know in our travels passed over many small rapids and cascades. Those pale in comparison with the foaming roaring fury of Great Falls where the Potomac drops 40 feet in about 600 feet and then runs through a narrow rock-walled gorge less than 80 feet wide in places.

The Power of the Potomac — Great Falls

At one point the river cascades down a 16-foot drop. We discovered that the foam created at the base of this drop was not natural but, rather, detergent suds - evidence of water pollution from towns and cities upstream. If you look closely near the base of some cliffs along the falls, you may think you are seeing some type of moss or lichen on the rocks. These rocks are covered with a metallic purplish tinge. This is really iron and manganese oxides staining the rocks. This stain is a result of acid mine drainage from coalmines in the upper Potomac River basin.

In the summer the flow of the Potomac through the falls may be less than 10,000 gallons a second, but during floods the flow commonly reaches 10 million gallons a second. The average flow pouring over the falls is 92,000 gallons of water every second.

With some quick calculations, Tom and I agreed that one year's worth of Potomac water would be equal to more than 2.5 trillion gallons. That is enough water to flood the entire District of Columbia to a depth of some 180 feet, converting the Washington Monument (555 feet high) into a tall lighthouse.

The same floods that damaged Paw Paw, Harpers Ferry, Williamsport, and other towns upstream also hit Great Falls. These floods have covered the towpath of the C&O Canal and spread across the area of the Visitor Center and parking lots on the Virginia side. While these floods are the exception rather than the norm, floods do hit the Great Falls area about once every 2 years. Floodwaters rise to the brink of the gorge at the falls and reach to within 13 to 20 feet of the trails and overlooks along the cliffs. The river along the main channel of Great Falls is normally about 33 feet deep. During the 1889 and 1936 floods the water was estimated to have been more than 100 feet deep. That left the parking lot area on the Virginia side of Great Falls under some 12 feet of water. A pole with high-water marks carved into it is at the Great Falls Visitor's Center on the Virginia side with the 1936 Flood notched at the very top.

The history of the Potomac as it courses its way over the falls is also a history of a time and places long forgotten. The birth of the Potomac came millions of years before Captain John Smith sailed up the river and named it "Pawtomack."

From when the Potomac was born, through the Civil War and the rebirth of the river after fighting man-made pollution, the Potomac has flowed unceasingly toward the sea. In our travels, there were many stretches of river where time seemed to stand still. As we floated past the tree-lined shores in the upper regions of the river, we found places where the date and time on our watches were of no importance. Had we slept like Rip Van Winkle along the banks of the Potomac, we would have been hard-pressed upon waking to figure out what year it was. Or even what decade. During the times when we did not use our outboard motor we were lazily pushed downstream by the river's current. We found ourselves daydreaming about when the world and the Potomac were formed.

We had seen evidence of what millions of years of constantly flowing water could do to a mountain. Yet there is no place like Great Falls to see how the constant flow of the river could strip away the soil and soft sandstone and cut into the harder underlying bedrock. Like detectives reconstructing the scene of some past event, we tried to analyze the obvious cracks and fractures in the bedrock. These bedrock succeeded in controlling and confining the movement of the river and laid bare a fascinating record of events stretching back millions of years.

We found that the average looking rocks exposed along the surface of the Potomac, or lying within reach of a shovel, was the source of our knowledge of early Potomac history. Geologists have read these samples and culled from them fascinating stories of vast cataclysmic upheavals of newly born mountains, tales of the movement of molten rocks through the Washington area, and images of ancient oceans and riverbeds.

We took a brief walk along the Potomac at Great Falls with a Forest Ranger. He showed us the obvious loss of soil and showed us five distinct kinds of bedrock: mica schist, metagraywacke, amphibolite, granite and lamprophyre. The mica schist, metagraywacke, and amphibolite were rocks, the Ranger said, that were buried deep within the earth's crust and transformed (metamorphosed) by heat and pressure to their present state. Before metamorphism the schists were mudstones or shales, the metagraywackes were beds of muddy sandstone, and the amphibolites were sheets of once-molten rock similar to basalt lava. How these formed are as much a history of the Potomac as they are the creation of the Earth.

Geological evidence suggests that about 4,600 million years ago a vast disc-like cloud of gas and dust condensed to form the star and planets we now know as the Solar System and a molten primeval glob now called Earth.

As the molten material solidified, gases, including water vapor, carbon dioxide and nitrogen were given off and began to build an atmosphere around the Earth. Water vapor condensed and fell as rain, starting the process still occurring today along the Potomac - that of erosion and sedimentation. This was 3,750 million years ago.

As the rains continued to fall, large bodies of water formed. The rain began separating the landmasses into individual continents that were then still moving fluidly around the globe. The hardened upper crust was still "floating" on molten rock. These continents would crack, collide into each other and reform into other landmasses. Two billion years ago, plant cells capable of photosynthesis had evolved enough from primitive living cells that they started adding oxygen to the atmosphere. By this time, all the major components of the Earth were present.

About 1,100 million years ago, clay-like shales and muddy sandstones were deposited on the bottom of an ancient long forgotten ocean, probably cascading down the steep eastern side of a deep trough near the coast of a rugged landmass that geologists call Euramerica. The muddy sandstones in the Potomac at Great Falls were formed probably when thick slurries of mud and sand moved downslope from the major rockslides and came to rest in the bottom of the trough. The shales of Great Falls were originally muddy sediments that were carried seaward by those long forgotten ocean currents. They settled to the bottom during the quiet intervals between the slides. Near Chain Bridge near Washington, D.C., the shale and sandstone deposits became so thickly packed that they began to heat up and melt from the pressure of the weight. Geologists say it "metamorphosed."

Soon after the shales and sandstones were deposited into the trough. Molten lava from the Earth's core, which had been injected in thick sheets parallel to the layers of deposit, cooled to form the layers of basalt that later become amphibolite. The high landmass from which these sediments were eroded has long been obliterated, but it probably lay only a few miles from Theodore Roosevelt Island located in the Potomac near Georgetown. It was made largely of granite-like rocks similar to those exposed today near Baltimore that has been determined by geologists to be about 1,100 million years old.

To hurry us back to the Great Falls of today, I'll jump 500 million years and talk about Earth 600 million years later. Earth was at the dawn of the Paleozoic Era, characterized by the appearance of plants, primitive fish and reptiles. This was the very beginning of the events that would create the Potomac River.

Six hundred million years ago, a great depression in the Earth's crust had formed that extended from present-day Newfoundland to Alabama called the Appalachian geosyncline. A broad, shallow sea then spread across this trough. Similar to 500 million years previously, erosional debris from ancient landmasses slowly gathered. Sediments accumulated in layers to a depth of several thousand feet, becoming compacted and cemented into sedimentary rocks. Sand particles formed sandstone and clay and silt combined to form shale. This time the decaying remains of primitive hard-skeleton plants and animals like corals and sponges turned into limestone.

The exact time the shale and sandstone sediments were deposited is uncertain because no fossils have been found in them. The dating of a rare radioactive mineral, zircon, suggests that the basalt layers were intruded with molten lava about 550 million years ago. The sediments are probably about the same age.

Since they were formed, these rocks have undergone a full and varied history. As younger sediments accumulated above them, they became more deeply buried. They were compressed, folded, metamorphosed, and finally intruded, or injected, by molten granite. The total thickness of sediment that accumulated can be deduced from laboratory geology experiments. Those tests show that some minerals that grew in the metamorphic rocks, called schists, reached temperatures of more than 1,200 degrees Fahrenheit and pressures corresponding to depths of 12 to 18 miles below the surface of the Earth when the granites were intruded. The exact age of this deformation and recrystallization is unknown, but dates determined for mica embedded in granite near Great Falls suggests that the granite was emplaced about 470 million years ago. Most of the deformation must have been done by that time.

Thus far in the history of these rocks, events were controlled by forces deep within the earth that led to the downbuckling of the sea floor, accumulation of sediments, and later, compression and folding. After the emplacement of granite, a fundamental change took place. The Earth's crust stopped moving down and slowly began to rise again, carrying the present day rocks at Great Falls, previously buried as far as 20 miles below the surface, back toward the Earth's surface. As the hardened crust rose upward from another series of upheavals, overlying rocks on the top of these huge mountains were eroded. The resulting debris was transported westward, where it accumulated as thick sedimentary deposits which now make up the main part of the Appalachian Mountains. Erosion was very rapid during the initial stages of the uplift, suggesting that the Piedmont area was very mountainous, perhaps much like the Rocky Mountains are today.

As erosion followed uplift, temperatures in the rocks gradually declined, and the rocks became fractured as they cooled. Evidence of these fractures is shown along the Potomac at Great Falls. Through some fractures, molten rock material of a different type rose from the Earth's core and solidified to form dark twisting sheets of lamprophyre. Dating of the minerals in the lamprophyre shows that they were intruded about 360 million years ago. Studies of ancient marine animals along lost coastlines have allowed a map to be drawn of how the Earth looked some 325 million years ago, including sea depths and sea-floor conditions. This is called the Carboniferous Epoch. Later, movement occurred along other fractures, shattering and crushing the rocks along them and displacing the rocks on either side. Zones along which such movements have taken place are called faults. The straight narrow section of the gorge below Rocky Islands in the Potomac is cut along one such fault. The Potomac River follows the fault zone because the broken rock along it is much more easily eroded than the unbroken rocks on either side.

Along some faults, hot solutions rose and deposited thick veins of white quartz. Some of these veins carry small amounts of gold that were mined sporadically around Great Falls from 1867 until as recently as 1941. Some panning continues along the banks of the Potomac River just east of the American Legion and the Cabin John Bridges. Many of these faults and quartz veins have the same orientation as faults of Triassic age (about 200 million years old) a few miles to the west. The faults at Great Falls may be of the same age.

The Triassic faults appear to have developed in response to one final stage of uplift, a regional arching and stretching of the Piedmont rocks, much like the arching of a cat's back when first waking. This arching produced a series of fault-bounded basins. These basins were filled with the red shales and sandstones that crop out a few miles west of Great Falls in the Leesburg Basin and Frederick Valley.

Further upstream from Great Falls, around the cliffs facing Harpers Ferry, is Weverton quartzite, a whitish rock with milky quartz grains.

About 275 million years ago three huge landmasses collided and fused into a single mass, creating mountain chains where they met. The Ural Mountains through the Soviet Union and the Alps mark the line of collision of two of these landmasses. About 230 million years ago, as the three landmasses were still pressing against each other, tremendous pressure exerted from the southeast drove the Earth's crust westward. This compressed the sedimentary strata of the Appalachian region into parallel faults and folds. Along the eastern edge of this area that geologists call a geosyncline, in an area extending from Virginia to Pennsylvania in a mostly north-south direction, this "Appalachian Revolution" forced up an immense fold in the earth's crust - the South Mountain anticlinorium. Imagine layers of different colored material all on top of one another, some the thickness of bedsheets, others as thick as carpeting. Now, push this pile across a newly waxed floor until it plows into the wall. If the pile is viewed sideways so that all the different colors and thickness can be seen, you can easily see how the Allegheny and Appalachian Mountains were formed. Short Mountain, Hill Mountain, Maryland Heights, Loudoun Heights, and Bolivar Heights are all smaller folds within this massive formation.

The tremendous forces that created these mountains subjected them to intense heat and pressure. Sedimentary rock metamorphosed, their internal structure being altered or changed altogether. In the Harpers Ferry area, sandstone became quartzite and shale became schist, slate or phyllite (Harpers shale). As the principal ridge-making elements here, these rock formations are accordion-pleated, tilted on end and uniformly rise westward.

Dinosaurs roamed the Potomac area 200 million years ago while this revolution was pushing the mountains higher. It was much quieter, geologically speaking, on the West Coast of the United States during this time. Most of the fossils of these huge beasts are found there, but tracings of them have been found in the Washington area and the Connecticut River valley. Specifically, discoveries have been made just south of Leesburg, Virginia, and at an excavation site at Culpeper, Virginia.

When James Monroe was president in 1820 he built a house just south of Leesburg, Virginia, which he named Oak Hill. He later wrote his famous Monroe Doctrine in the house that his friend Thomas Jefferson and architect James Hoban helped design. In the early 1920s, the owner of the home decided to add gardens, walkways and outdoor terraces in keeping with Monroe's original plans, which Monroe had never finished. Stonemasons used the outcropping of slate and shale on the property as the source of the flagstone slabs needed for the new construction. There they found odd markings on the slate, which were authenticated as dinosaur footprints, hide marks and tail draggings some 200 million years old. Two hundred million years ago, Earth had one continent geologists call Pangaea. Carnivorous reptiles and some of the first dinosaurs to rule the land populated it. In an open quarry being mined in Culpeper, over 900 dinosaur footprints have been found. In the ocean, sharks had appeared.

The region around the District of Columbia was still under water. An area now along the Potomac River called Horsehead Cliffs in Westmoreland State Park in Virginia gives us great insight into how underwater life existed there 5 to 15 million years ago.

The sea began to withdraw eastward from the Washington area between 6 and 7 million years ago, and the land was slowly pushed upward. As it pushed upward, streams draining from the Appalachians spread a blanket of silt, sand and gravel over the coastal and Piedmont areas. A single major river did not lay down this blanket, but by many streams that constantly shifted their courses back and forth to form a complex series of fan-shaped deposits of sand and gravel. Remnants of this blanket are preserved today, capping some of the highest hills in the Piedmont near the Tysons Corner shopping center in Virginia - 518 feet above sea level. Imagine what a garden hose does when you turn the water on - it whips back and forth across the ground until you race across the yard and pick it up. Imagine this process of whipping back and forth slowed over many years. This is what happened with the streams as the land rose up and changed the stream's path.

The slow rise of the Piedmont and the Appalachians to the west continued and increased the slope of the land surface. This caused the streams to deepen their valleys and eventually to combine into a river that was to become the Potomac. The Potomac waters then deepened the valley and scattered remnants of

its former flood plains were left at various levels as gravel covered terraces. About 2 million years ago, the river had carved a broad open valley in approximately its present position.

When the Earth's climate cooled, great amounts of water became trapped in the expanding polar ice caps and the level of the oceans began to drop. With the beginning of the continental glaciation that occurred during the Pleistocene Epoch - about 2 million years ago - the sea level was lowered. The Potomac River began deepening the early valleys it had made when the land was pushed upwards. When the water withdrew from the oceans to form the great ice sheets on the land, sea levels around the world fell by as much as 500 feet. Most of the continental shelf off the Eastern United States was exposed, and the shoreline lay as much as 400 miles east of its present position. Continental glaciation occurred not just once, but at least 4 times in the last 2 million years. The last glacier advanced into central New Jersey as recently as 18,000 years ago, and glaciers disappeared from much of Canada only about 12,000 years ago.

As the sea level fell, the Potomac River cut correspondingly deeper depressions into the floor of its valley. The valley rapidly deepened in the Great Falls area because this area was composed of soft, easily eroded materials such as sandstone. In the hard rocks of the Piedmont, the erosion caused by the increased flow of the water, called downcutting, was much slower. It was this eventual downcutting from the sandstone into the hard bedrock floor of the older wider valley that produced the spectacular rocky gorge of the Potomac River between Little Falls and Great Falls. At Great Falls the river encounters a series of thick rock layers that are particularly resistant to downcutting and erosion. These hard ledges have slowed the progress of valley cutting. The river above Great Falls thus remains essentially the unmodified, original pre-Pleistocene valley, but below the falls the river flows in a gorge excavated within the last 2 million years. Along the gorge the original valley floor can be recognized as a flat and level gravel-covered stretch of land 18 to 60 feet above the present river level. Geologists call this stretch a bench. MacArthur Boulevard in Washington, D.C., and suburban Maryland follows this bench from Cabin John Run to the Old Anglers Inn.

The landscape all along the 383-mile length of the Potomac River is the result of a continuing struggle between the deep-seated earth forces that raised the land above sea level and the forces of erosion that gradually wore down the land surface.

Erosion along the Potomac begins with the weathering of rocks - the chemical decay and solution of mineral grains and the mechanical disintegration of rocks by frost. The resulting debris is carried into the streams and rivers flowing into the Potomac, aided by frost actions and the slow creep of soil from the farmlands down the slopes. Once in the streams the debris is transported into the Potomac. From there, seaward, either dissolved in the Potomac waters; or as mud and silt in suspension; or as sand, gravel and boulders that are rolled and bounced along the bottom. The Potomac River is estimated to carry more than 1.6 million tons of sediment and about 1.1 million tons of dissolved material seaward each year. This amounts to 142 tons of material removed from each square mile of the river's drainage basin above Great Falls.

Today the Potomac, like other Atlantic seaboard rivers, rises in the Appalachian Mountains and flows eastward to the Atlantic Ocean. As we have already seen, the Potomac perks through the ground at the Fairfax Stone in West Virginia, runs northwest to Cumberland, Maryland, cuts through the Blue Ridge at a narrow gap below Harpers Ferry and across Catoctin Mountain, the easternmost ridge of the Appalachians, and through a similar gap at Point of Rocks. From there to its mouth, the river flows across three more major landscape provinces: a broad lowland between Point of Rocks and Seneca that is called the Frederick Valley in Maryland and the Leesburg Basin in Virginia; the Piedmont between Seneca and Washington; and the Coastal between Washington and Point Lookout.

The nature of the landscape and Potomac River valley in each of these provinces is determined largely by the nature of the underlying rocks. Principally red sandstone and shale that were deposited during the Triassic and Jurassic Periods, about 200 million years ago, underlie the Frederick Valley. Because these rocks are eroded, the land's surface is nearly flat, with slopes that are gentle and smooth. The Potomac River is much like the Mississippi River: wide, sluggish, and shallow, and is flanked by broad flats frequently covered by floodwaters.

The Piedmont is a rolling, hilly upland underlain by hard rocks. Although these rocks are very resistant to erosion, they are subject to chemical decay. This decay extends at places to depths of 100 feet or more and produces saprolite (rotten rock) and deep red clay-embedded soils. The smaller streams on the uplands have not cut through the blanket of solid and soft decayed rock and thus flow in broad valleys and wide flood plains. However, the larger streams have cut through to hard rocks and flow within narrow steep-sided valleys having constricted flood plains.

The nature of the Potomac Plateau is variable. Above Great Falls the valley is steep but wide and in most places the river is broad, shallow, and placid. In a few places, riffles and rapids break the quiet water as it passes across shoals and resistant ledges of rock. The many islands are composed of sand and gravel laid down by the river. None of them rise much above the level of the flood that occurs about every 2 years. At Great Falls the character of the river changes abruptly. From Great Falls to Theodore Roosevelt Island it flows within a series of narrow rock-girded channels twisting between cliffs and flat-topped bedrock islands that rise above the level of the highest known floods. After Great Falls, the Potomac passes over a series of other rapids and falls, including Yellow Falls, Stubblefield Falls, and Little Falls. The river then reaches the tidal flows of the sea at Chain Bridge.

As the river flows beneath the Arlington Memorial Bridge, it leaves the Piedmont and enters the Coastal area. Layered deposits of sand, clay, gravel and shells underlie the Coastal area. These were laid down in and along the edge of the sea when it encroached onto the eastern edge of the continent at various times during the past 100 million years. In cross section, these deposits resemble a gigantic wedge ranging in thickness from a few meters near the Theodore Roosevelt Island's edge to nearly 10,000 feet along the Maryland coast. Chesapeake Bay and its system of estuaries are ancient valleys cut in the soft sediments of the Coastal Plain when sea level stood much lower. When the sea rose to its present level, the valleys were flooded. The Potomac River occupies one of these "drowned" valleys between Washington and its mouth at Point Lookout. The broad river, influenced by tides and navigable by oceangoing ships, is flanked by wide low terraces and, in a few places, by wave-carved bluffs in the soft Coastal Plain rocks.

The boundary between the hard rocks of the Piedmont and the soft, easily eroded rocks of the Coastal area is called the Fall Line. It is the Fall Line along which falls and rapids are encountered in ascending the major rivers. It marks the head of navigation for oceangoing ships and the farthest point downstream that fords or small bridges can cross the streams. Many cities of the eastern seaboard from Trenton, New Jersey, to Macon, Georgia, including Washington, D.C., were established along or near the Fall Line.

It was along this Fall Line that the restless spirit of adventurism, and entrepreneurism, took hold. Archeological excavations conducted in the area where the Kennedy Center is revealed five different cultural periods of American Indian occupation from 500 B.C.

to A.D. 1700. Then the Europeans arrived and began settling down in the Washington, D.C., area. Many early settlers, tired with the increasing population, laws, taxes, began to move westward across the land, through virgin forests and clear streams. Many records of their journeys expressed satisfaction that the waters of the Potomac ran so clear.

While most early settlers populated the country along the East Coast and into New England, many soon began moving up the rivers in search of a more agrarian lifestyle. Along the rivers they found tillable farmland, or they felled trees along the rivers to make farmland. These farmers crept along the Mississippi, the Great Lakes, and the Potomac. Some boldly moved into the mid-West where the productivity of the land to raise grain and cattle was immeasurable. Two of these areas close by are called the Shenandoah Valley and the Ohio Valley. During the rush to claim land toward California and the ensuing gold rush, many simply stopped and settled in the mid-West. As we developed into a larger nation, the problem of transportation became apparent. The commercial and maritime areas of the East and Gulf coasts had to be joined to the productive territories further west. Better and cheaper means of transportation were needed to move the goods, grain and raw materials. Waterways were ideal although at times they could not be trusted to provide the depth or current needed to move these materials safely by barge. That meant that something had to be built to control and tame the waters. And that meant canals. George Washington was the first to try out this idea with the Potowmack Canal Company,

and he began at what is today the Great Falls Park on the Virginia side.

The Potowmack Company was formed in 1784 to construct a series of five canals on the Virginia side to make the Potomac River navigable. George Washington presided over the effort, a dream of his since his youth when he surveyed the river and its tributaries. Washington was convinced that such canals would stimulate trade between the east and the Ohio Valley, bind the country together in a framework of trade and mutual interest.

Construction began on this Patowmack canal system—America's first—in 1785 and was completed in 1802. The canals at Little Falls above Georgetown and at Great Falls both required locks, a challenge for the engineers of the company. Skirting canals, to better control the boats instead of running them through too shallow or too swift moving water, were dug at Seneca Falls and at Harpers Ferry. Elsewhere, the company simply dredged and improved the existing riverbed.

In 1790 the town of Matildaville was sponsored by "Light Horse Harry" Lee, a Revolutionary War General and friend of Washington. The town, near Great Falls, flourished for nearly three decades but declined in the 1820s as trade dwindled.

Later George Washington and others conceived the C&O Canal to link the Potomac waterway with the rich Shenandoah and Ohio River valleys. This was a project considered absolutely necessary for the survival of Georgetown and Alexandria as ports. In 1828 the Chesapeake and Ohio Canal Company bought the old Potowmack Canal and its rights, eventually linking the city of Washington with a continuous canal. The C&O Canal was one of the first "highways" to the west, and Tom and I had been floating parallel to the canal since Cumberland. The C&O Canal soon lost to the Baltimore & Ohio Railroad, which could carry larger loads faster and less expensively than the canal barges.

Across from the remains of the Potowmack Canal at Great Falls lie Falls Island and Olmstead Island. When Tom and I were on the Maryland side we watched as kayakers reached the rapids known at Wet Bottom Chute. While not being able to figure out how and why these islands got their names, Tom and I did agree that some twisted demented kayakers must have named the rapids. Wet Bottom Chute was an aptly deserved name. I did discover that Olmstead Island was named after the landscape architect Frederick Law Olmstead. As we walked further downstream along the Virginia shoreline we reached Mather Gorge. From the Maryland side you reached Mather Gorge by walking on the well-named Billy Goat Trail on Bear Island. Mather Gorge was named after Stephen T. Mather (1867-1930), first director of the National Park Service (1917-1929). Mather helped shape America's National Park System, a philosophy of conservation that was spread throughout the world.

While we watched kayakers get swept down the 1-1/2 mile length of Mather Gorge, we felt more comfortable observing and taking photographs from our overlook on Bear Island. Bear Island is not really an island at all, but only separated from the Maryland mainland by the Potomac waters of the C&O canal

Exercising On the Potomac—Rock Climbers at Great Falls

and an area called Widewater. The island hangs onto the Maryland shore and during many floods that sweep down the river, Bear Island really does become an island. In a few floods it has altogether disappeared, although now the river flows some 40 feet below us. Those not wearing a pair of good hiking boots or other non-skid footwear soon figures out why it's called the Billy Goat Trail. Even in my hiking boots, I can highly recommend avoiding wet or icy rocks along this trail. Trust me.

At one point Tom and I found ourselves leaning over a Bear Island precipice straight down into Mather Gorge. We were lining up camera shots of kayakers in the river. I was thinking about using this as an excellent example of the Venturi Effect, Italian physicist G. B. Venturi's discovery - that is: as the area in which a fluid is travelling is constricted, velocity of the fluid increases. Upstream, the Potomac had been formed by the drainage of nearly 15,000 square miles of territory, if tributaries such as the Shenandoah River are included. At Mather Gorge, all the Potomac waters that had been spilling over the various falls gather again and try to get through this single constricted area. According to Venturi, the fluid should speed up. It does, and dramatically, if you lean over far enough to see it. That's when my foot slipped on the rocks and I nearly lost my balance.

The granddaddy of all boulders pushed along by the Potomac is now sitting high and dry - almost exactly one mile downstream and along the walk path from the south entrance of the Virginia Great Falls Park. All along the trail are rounded pebbles, cobbles, and boulders left behind by the river when it flowed at this level. This one boulder is 5 feet in diameter and estimated to weigh over 4.4 tons! It is composed of dark, igneous rock called diabase. The nearest outcrop of diabase is near Blockhouse Point, 7 miles upstream. This boulder is far too large to have been moved by even the largest modern flood. Could it have floated on an ice jam or in a tangle of felled and floating trees?

Unlikely. It more than likely suggests even larger and more violent floods that occurred in this area at one time, possibly thousands of years ago.

Passing the boulder and coming to the bottom of the gorge, at 1.3 miles downstream from the Virginia Visitors Center at Great Falls Park, we came across the remnants of a disaster long past. While the Potomac may be capable of turning left 90 degrees at this point and rushing toward the Maryland side of the river, many items floating on the river get stuck at the turn. Here there is an abundant amount of flood debris piled up in the nook of the river. Trees felled by Hurricane Agnes in June 1972 are now dead and scattered at least 50 feet higher than today's water level, which was running at normal level.

Another item we discovered were round holes in the larger rocks. We learned that these were made by nature are called, ironically enough, potholes. While this may have been the origin meaning of the word "pothole," the word is now used to depict the state of some of our roads and bridges. Potholes are naturally formed circular holes ground into the larger rocks by pebbles churned by the swirling currents of the river when it flowed at that higher level. The current was not strong enough to push the rocks out of the depression in the stone, so the pebbles simply swirled about in a circular motion. Circling, they slowly ground away at the rock beneath them. As the hole became deeper, larger rocks would drop in and continue the process.

After the river turns, it rushes past Sherwin Island on the left, then after about one-third of a mile, makes another abrupt 90 degree turn, this time to the right.

Right after the turn is the put-in for kayakers who start at the Old Angler's Inn.

We watched as kayakers maneuvered their way through the swirling waters and around the islands - Offut, Hermit, Herzog, Turkey and Vaco - all guarding the Carderock-Cropley area of the C&O Canal National Historical Park. The trail we were on brought us right down to the river and allowed us to follow the shoreline and the kayakers very closely. This was due, in part, to the laborers who built a remarkable stone wall in 1830 extending about 60 feet high and several hundred feet in length to support the C&O Canal and its towpath.

The Calico Rapids flow around to the left of Turkey Island while Yellow Falls greets the kayakers taking the right side. In either case, they meet up again before rushing through Stubblefield Falls. The falls can be viewed from a delightful park across the street from the David W. Taylor Naval Ship Research and Development Center at Carderock, Maryland. One of the buildings at the Center looks like a very long Quonset hut. Inside is a 2,600-foot long "swimming pool" or basin used to test ship models.

From the Virginia side this area is called the Dranesville District Park. The park is a 336-acre preserve bordering the Potomac from Scott Run to the American Legion Bridge. It was one of our last visits along this section of the Potomac. This area is a rolling upland forest with high bluffs and a narrow floodplain. Administered by the Fairfax County Park Authority, the area has been left almost undisturbed; a network of well-established but unmarked trails provides access to most of the park. Outstanding attractions of Dranesville District Park are the trail along the palisades of the Potomac and the gorge at the lower end of Scott Run that announces its arrival to the Potomac with a small waterfall. At the lower end of the park are the Stubblefield Falls surrounded by large hemlocks and polypody ferns.

The last item of interest before heading under the American Legion Bridge is a small stream flowing into the Potomac from Maryland called Rock Run. This stream flowed into the Potomac nearly a mile downstream from the American Legion Bridge, instead of the present-day course a quarter mile upstream from the bridge. What accounts for this one-and-a-quarter mile difference between the same stream shown on recent charts of the area? The answer is: "man." The stream was diverted because of the complications it was making during the construction of the present day Beltway (Interstate 495) that crosses over the American Legion Bridge. It was simpler for the engineers to block the natural flow of the stream and divert it in another direction than to work around it and pour concrete foundations for the Beltway into the path of the water.

Tom Sherman

CHAPTER 4

From the American Legion Bridge to the Woodrow Wilson Bridge

After crashing through Great Falls, the Potomac River changes drastically. We began this portion of our journey just under the American Legion Bridge. While often confused with the Cabin John Bridge nearby, the American Legion Bridge is one of two places where the Capitol Beltway and the Potomac River intersect. Woodrow Wilson Bridge is the other intersection that, coincidentally, concludes this chapter.

The very item of interest on the narrow Potomac River just past the American Legion Bridge is Plummers Island, hugging the Maryland shoreline. Now owned by the National Park Service, the Washington Biologists' Field Club has used this island since 1901. It is said that this island has been more intensively studied than any other area of comparable size in the United States.

Opposite Plummers Island on the Virginia side was once the site of a ferry to the low area across the Potomac. During the early operation of the Potowmack Canal, when all improvements had been made except the completion of the locks at Great Falls, goods from upriver were portaged around the falls to Washington's Pawtomack Canal on the Virginia side and loaded into barges to continue the trip downstream. Now, the area is an improved gravel road used by rescue and recovery vehicles when saving lives or pulling bodies from the rapids.

Just past Plummers Island, Cabin John Creek flows out of a wooded valley and into the Potomac from upper Maryland, just upstream from Glen Echo. The river and an aqueduct just upstream from the

creek are interesting enough to abandon the boats and hike back to the aqueduct. The aqueduct is north of the American Legion Bridge.

The Cabin John Bridge, originally called the Union Arch, is confused sometimes with the American Legion Bridge, due to years of airborne traffic reporters referring to only the Cabin John Bridge when making their traffic report of that area.

What some motorists may not know is that what they are driving under may be the longest stone arch bridge in the world. Over a hundred years ago, the Washington area depended upon creeks, springs and public wells and pumps for its water supply. Pulling water directly out of the Potomac was never that healthy. This worked fine until the population of Washington grew - a new source of water in a much larger volume had to be found. That is when, in 1853, General Montgomery C. Meigs of the Army Corps of Engineers planned an aqueduct to bring water from the Great Falls to the city. To bring the water over the deep valley of Cabin John Run, he built a 220-foot red sandstone bridge. The Union Arch still today carries the water line over the Cabin John Creek Valley.

The red sandstone came from the Seneca Sandstone Quarry and Stone-Cutting Mill just west of Seneca Creek above Great Falls.

When the aqueduct was authorized by Congress, Franklin Pierce was president, albeit a president of the Confederacy but the president of our country nonetheless. Jefferson Davis was secretary of war and soon after became another president of the Confederacy. When the waterway was finished,

Abraham Lincoln was president. Unknown to most of the motorists sitting on the bridge above, there is a large plaque installed on the bridge abutment to commemorate this engineering achievement.

After the outbreak of the Civil War, the Secretary of the Interior (Why is the person charged with protecting the National Parks and the great outdoors of the United States called the Secretary of the Interior?) was horrified to see the name of Jefferson Davis on the same memorial as that of Abraham Lincoln. He ordered Davis's name chiseled away, and for years after the war there was a blank line on the plaque. Descendants of Jefferson Davis and other sympathetic groups protested this insult and lobbied vigorously to have the name put back. Finally, President Theodore Roosevelt ordered a new plaque made to include the names of both Davis and Lincoln. The plaque with both names is there today on the Cabin John Aqueduct Bridge. It is perhaps the only place in the nation where the names of the president of the United States and the president of the Confederacy appear together.

Some say that "Cabin John" is a corruption of "Captain John"; that is, if you say "Captain John" enough times it does begin to sound like "Cabin John." The Captain John referred to here is, as the legend goes, Captain John Smith of Potomac (and Pocahontas) fame. Another legend is that a Captain John ran a ferry across the Potomac at this point before any bridges were built. Another legend says that an early settler who people called John of the Cabin found gold in the creek and that for years deeds to land near what is now Cabin John Bridge required

purchasers to surrender part of any gold treasure found on the property.

Across from Cabin John along the Virginia side is the Dead Run-Turkey Run area. The Dead Run to Turkey Run area includes the valley of Turkey Run from Turkey Run Road down to the Potomac waters along the Virginia shoreline. The land runs along the Potomac between Turkey Run and Dead Run, and the Dead Run ravine runs back to the George Washington Memorial Parkway. This area essentially is undeveloped and the variety of spring wildflowers is worth the trip, either viewed from along the shore from a small boat or on foot. We saw hikers traversing the various springs feeding into the Potomac along the shore using stepping-stones. The lower ravine of Dead Run is scenic, with rocky cascades.

The whitewater begins to appear after Turkey Run pours out into the Potomac. As the river narrows, the whitewater soon turns frantic and doesn't let up for nearly a half-mile until you pass Sycamore Island hard against the Maryland shore. Back on the whitewater, it is interesting that you are passing an historical town along the Maryland shore. The town is Glen Echo.

Glen Echo began as a resort in 1889, becoming the site of the "National Chautauqua" or "Chautauqua Meeting Ground," a utopian community. The Chatauqua Tower in Glen Echo Park is a partially restored reminder of the utopian era that hit the brick wall of reality when the 1892 malaria epidemic struck. Indian names such as Walhounding Road originated in the days of the Chautauqua movement. Glen Echo sprang back to life in 1911 when it became an amusement park, drawing thousands of Washingtonians, many of them coming by trolley from Georgetown. The trolley rails are still visible along the C&O Canal. The National Park Service operates the park as an arts center. While the name 'Echo' was just someone's fancy, the word 'Glen' appropriately suggests the gullies of this scenic hilly area. Nearby, the Clara Barton House, also operated by the National Park Service, is an interesting large framed building on the bluff overlooking the Potomac. This house was for many years the home of Clara Barton and headquarters of that famous organization she created, the American Red Cross. The house was built in 1892 from wood taken from the Red Cross barracks at Johnstown, Pennsylvania; the Red Cross barracks used to house refugees after the 1889 flood. The house is designed in the style of a Mississippi riverboat. The front middle windows of the third story contain panes of red glass arranged, as you may well guess, into the familiar Red Cross pattern. Clara died in this house in 1912 at the age of 91, having survived to help the wounded in 19 Civil War battles and 9 Franco-Prussian War battles. The nearby highway that runs parallel with the Potomac River on the Maryland side was renamed the Clara Barton Memorial Highway.

When you make it through that whitewater, it is time to pull your boat back out of the water, because a killer dam is ahead. It is called Little Falls Dam, or Dam Number 1 and it is also the location of the Little Falls Pumping Station. Little Falls passes High Island on its left as it runs downstream, and on it

right, hidden by homes and trees, is a Civil War fort called Fort Marcy.

A walk through the fort will allow you to catch a glimpse of the river, as you stand surrounded by cannon dispersed through the area. Fort Marcy guarded the Virginia approaches to the Chain Bridge on what was called the old Leesburg Turnpike and by Fort Ethan Allen on the Military Road. The sites were occupied by Union troops on September 24th, 1861, and the earthworks completed shortly afterward. Fort Marcy was named for Brigadier General Randolph B. Marcy, Chief of Staff for Major General George B. McClellan. The armament consisted of 17 guns with one platform vacant and three mortars.

With little fanfare, the Potomac slips past the invisible line separating Montgomery County, Maryland, from the District of Columbia. Here one can walk out onto a viewing area to watch the hundreds of people fishing and a few kayakers handling the calmer waters past Little Falls. Just downstream from the viewing area is Chain Bridge.

In 1797, the first bridge over the Potomac was constructed. Built by the Georgetown Bridge Company, the bridge was called The Falls Bridge. The bridge collapsed in 1810 after only 13 years and a new bridge was built - this time suspended from iron chains made of links that were each 4-and-1/2 feet long. As a result, the bridge quickly became known as "Chain Bridge." The original Chain Bridge lasted until 1852 when it also collapsed. A heavy wooden crossbeam bridge replaced it during the Civil War, but its name was retained.

During the Civil War, the bridge served as the link between Union troops in Fairfax County and their Reserves remaining in Washington. In 1874 the wooden bridge was considered unsafe and torn down and another bridge built in its place. Major repairs were made on this bridge in 1927; just in time to have the bridge ripped apart by the 1936 flood. By 1938 a new and higher bridge, the one you see today, opened to the commuting public.

On the Virginia side at this point along the Potomac is the Potomac Overlook Regional Park, a 100-acre nature-oriented reservation. The Northern Virginia Regional Park Authority manages it. The name is misleading - since trees have grown up in front of the overlook to destroy the view of the Potomac. You can only really see the Potomac in the winter when the leaves have fallen off the trees. Archeological digs have confirmed that Indians lived in this area for many centuries. An old Indian spring can still be seen along one of the trails. Directly across the river from the overlook is Fletcher's Boat House where people rent boats to float on the Potomac. Downstream a bit we came in sight of Key Bridge, but before we passed under it, we passed by Three Sisters Islands, which is a story all by itself.

During the reign of King George, the king granted a parcel of land to John Moore. Part of this estate included Three Sisters Islands. According to an ancient legend repeated in the October 4, 1907, issue of the McLean Providence Journal newspaper, Three Sisters Islands received its name because three Analostan Indian sisters were riding in a frail craft at night that capsized on the Potomac due to a whirlpool. The three sisters drowned off the rocks of the little islands. As late as 1820 these islands had an aggregate soil surface of about four acres and were considered one of the finest fishing spots on the Potomac. Fishing continues, but the islands have been reduced to a pile of hard rocks sticking up out of the river, the soil and soft sandstone gone.

We motored past the remains of the Alexandria Canal Aqueduct and the Potomac Boat Club on the Maryland shore. We passed under the Francis Scott Key Bridge that connects Rosslyn, Virginia with Georgetown in Washington, D.C. Ahead the river forked around Theodore Roosevelt Island. Silhouetted against the sky above our heads along the Washington horizon was the Washington National Cathedral. Ahead of us was the unmistakable Washington Harbour with its fountains and columns; we had made it to Georgetown.

Georgetown began as a seaport, a trading center, and a residential area. It was a city whose name was authorized by the Maryland Provincial Assembly in 1751 to be just "George," but soon thereafter was called Georgetown. It became a neighborhood for low income workers and was revived as a prestigious, chic area with high-cost homes and expensive shops and restaurants.

The first non-Indian visitor to Georgetown was Captain John Smith who sailed up the Potomac as far as the Little Falls in 1608. He thought the place delightful. By the middle of the 18th Century, Georgetown was a small collection of homes, taverns and warehouses that owed their existence to the great Maryland and Virginia commodity, tobacco.

The original survey in 1752 plotted a city of 60 acres from what is now 30th Street to Georgetown University and from N Street to the river. The two men on whose farmland the city was established grumbled mightily but accepted in compensation 280 pounds and two city lots. There were only 80 lots in the whole town.

John Carroll, the first Roman Catholic Bishop in America, founded the Georgetown Academy in 1789. From that grew the Georgetown College and later the Georgetown University of today. Georgetown College was here before the District of Columbia. If you translate the Latin legend on Georgetown University's seal, "Collegium Georgeopolitanum ad ripas Potomici in Marylandia," it reads "Georgetown College on the banks of the Potomac in Maryland." Georgetown was the first of many colleges and universities now in the D.C. area.

Historians generally agree that the original thought of having an area such as the District of Columbia came about at a meeting of the Congress in June 1783 in the Old City Hall in Philadelphia, Pennsylvania. The War for Independence was over but it had also cleaned out the treasury. The young country lacked a president and had no lines of credit to foreign banks. Its military was not being paid, and all 13 colonies were about to go their separate ways. These priorities which Congress had before them where quickly set aside when, on June 20th, 1783, a large group of unpaid soldiers marched into Philadelphia to present their grievances to Congress. After calm was restored, many Congressmen started a petition to establish a federal area within the United States where they could conduct the business of government without fear of intimidation. Several places were suggested, but the Northern and Southern Congressmen didn't agree on any of them. Reaching several compromises, the Congressmen elected a president, George Washington, and placed the ultimate decisions into his hands.

Before Tom and I reached Theodore Roosevelt Island, we slipped past the canyon of buildings called Rosslyn, Virginia. Rosslyn was named for its 1860 landowner, William Henry Ross. Here you can see the airfoil-style twin buildings of the Gannett Building, better known as the USA Today building, easily seen by passengers out the right-hand windows as they descend into Ronald Reagan National Airport-bound. And those in the building can easily see the aircraft. On particularly foggy days, employees in the buildings have been known to dive under their desks at the sound of a descending aircraft. The precedent of aircraft flying in the area of Rosslyn had already been set at Fort Myer, site of the first heavier-then-air flight in Virginia.

It was at Fort Myer that Orville and Wilbur Wright had to prove that their airplane, the A-1, could fly two persons at the altitude and distance required by contract. Orville Wright made history by piloting the first heavier-than-air flight in Virginia at Fort Myer on September 4, 1908. A United States Army Signal Corps log noted the flight spanned three miles at a height of 40 feet. The flight of 4 minutes and 15 seconds was described as "good."

On September 9, 1908, Orville Wright carried aloft in public his first passenger, Lt. Frank P. Lahm, for a flight lasting six minutes and 24 seconds. Three days later, he took Major George O. Squier on a flight lasting nine minutes and six seconds duration.

On October 3, 1908, Orville won a coin toss and chose to fly the fragile craft; he kept it aloft for 71 seconds. Two weeks later, Orville took a passenger, Army Lt. Thomas Selfridge. The plane was aloft for four minutes when a propeller broke and the plane lost control. Wright was injured in the crash, and Selfridge died of injuries sustained. Later, the Wrights won the contract when they launched from the highest hill at Fort Myer, flew down to Alexandria, Virginia, and returned.

There is no mention of Selfridge's claim to fame as the world's first heavier-than-air passenger casualty.

Rosslyn has another claim to fame, but no one could really tell by today's Potomac. Five hundred million years ago, Great Falls' roaring waters were pouring over what is called the Fall Line at Rosslyn. Today, the Potomac waters have all but cut away into the soft sandstone and rocks to turn the distance between Rosslyn and the current location of Great Falls into a somewhat shallower and broader ravine.

Except for the Alexandria waterfront (Old Town), most of the Potomac shoreline in Virginia from Rosslyn to Occoquan Bay is publicly owned. The George Washington Memorial Parkway follows the Virginia shore from the American Legion Bridge to Mount Vernon. A bike path is open from the Theodore Roosevelt Island to Mount Vernon.

We had a decision to make as we approached Theodore Roosevelt Island: float to the left of the island and remain in the main Potomac River, or go to the right and into Little River. We split the difference and Tom and I came ashore on the most northerly point of land we saw on the island. We almost didn't make it. The high tide must have hidden from our view the wooden pilings with its rusted nails sticking out. We again ripped a two-inch gash in the bottom of the inflatable before getting ashore. Once on shore we saw a sign that read that a wooden bridge once connected the island with the mainland. The remains of that bridge must have cut the inflatable. Originally known as Analostan Island, this island has had a series of owners and names. After 1632, Charles I granted the island to Lord Baltimore and the island became known as "My Lord's Island." The next owner, Captain Randolph Brandt, purchased the island in 1681 and named it after his home in the West Indies: "Barbadoes." George Mason purchased the island in 1717. John Mason inherited it in 1792 and built a brick home here, converting the island to a fine farm estate. The Masons owned the island for 125 years and it became "Mason's Island." After the Civil War the island was owned by the Columbia Athletic Association, the Analostan Boat Club, and the Washington Gas Light Company. The Theodore Roosevelt Memorial Association in 1931 finally acquired it, and the following year was presented to the Nation. The memorial was dedicated on October 27,

1967. The 88-acre island in the middle of the Potomac is managed by the National Park Service and stands as a memorial to the conservation achievements of our 26th President. On the island is a 17-foot bronze statue of the president, surrounded by a circular path by four giant blocks of granite. Each 21 foot high block is inscribed with different memorable quotes chiseled into the blocks - Roosevelt's Philosophy of Citizenship. These tenets are interesting and we walked around reading them all:

manhood. A man's usefulness depends upon his living up to his ideals in so far as he can. It is hard to fail, but it is worse never to have tried to succeed. All daring and courage, all iron endurance of misfortune make for a finer and nobler type of manhood. Only those are fit to live who do not fear to die; and none are fit to die who have shrunk from the joy of life and the duty of life.

youth. I want to see you game, boys, I want to see you brave and manly, but I also want to see you gentle and tender. Be practical as well as generous in your ideals. Keep your eyes on the stars, but remember to keep your feet on the ground. Courage, hard work, self-mastery, and intelligent effort are all essential to successful life. Alike for the Nation and the individual, the one indispensable requisite is character.

the state. Ours is a government of liberty by, through, and under the law. A great democracy has got to be progressive or it will soon cease to be great or a democracy. Order without liberty and liberty without order are equally destructive. In popular government results worth having can be achieved only by men who combine worthy ideals with practical good sense. If I must choose between righteousness and peace I choose righteousness.

It was the last one we read that really struck home and to me it summed up the reason we were doing this book:

nature. There is delight in the hardy life of the open. There are no words that can tell the hidden spirit of the wilderness that can reveal its mystery, its melancholy, and its charm. The Nation behaves well if it treats the natural resources as assets which it must turn over to the next generation increased and not impaired in value. Conservation means development as much as it does protection.

We were to visit the island again, and it was a visit that almost got us arrested. We spent a few hours on the island, and had first walked south to see the Theodore Roosevelt Bridge up close.

We continued around to the eastern side of the island, and found what we were looking for. We were facing the Potomac waters and looking over at the John F. Kennedy Center for the Performing Arts, and Watergate. With tripods set up, we clicked away as sunset approached - the dying light turning the clouds and the 630 feet of white Carrara marble of the Center to pink. As it grew darker, a person rowed a skiff past us, heading upstream to the Potomac Boat Club. Then it was dark, and we were taking postcard-perfect photographs of the Kennedy Center with its reflection of lights in the Potomac. Then we packed up and headed for the car, only to be met by a couple of National Park

Entertainment Along the Potomac — Kennedy Center at Dusk with Watergate

Service police. They looked like this had happened once too often lately, and the Arlington County Police were ready to haul us off to jail. The park, as with most parks administered by the National Park Service, close and lock their gates at sunset. Between summer and winter, that's a difference in closing time of some four hours, and it just didn't occur to us that we would be locked inside. They waited for us with growing impatience, was ready to administer their particular form of justice to us by sending us off with the county police. Some quick talking and we were sent away with a warning. We got some great photographs, and Tom took the best of the Kennedy Center shots and turned it into a painting.

Later, the United States Marine Corps War Memorial, better known as the Iwo Jima Memorial, was the next sight for us to see from our boat. The memorial is a sculpture of the famous photograph taken by Joe Rosenthal showing the raising of the American flag on Mount Suribachi on February 23, 1945. The memorial has become known as a symbol of this Nation's esteem for the honored dead of the U.S. Marine Corps. It is interesting that one of the men helping to raise the flag is a Navy Corpsman. It is also interesting that this is the largest sculpture ever cast in bronze. Next to the memorial is the Netherlands Carillon. This 49-bell carillon was a gift from the Dutch in appreciation for the support the United States provided in World War I.

As we drifted under the Arlington Memorial Bridge, Tom was trying to line up a passing between the Lincoln Memorial and us. We passed under Memorial Bridge, a bridge built in the neo-classical design and designated as the northern terminus of the Mount Vernon Memorial Highway. The highway is more commonly known as the George Washington Memorial Parkway.

Near the area where the Memorial Bridge was built, an eccentric writer named Anne Royall finally succeeded in her quest to obtain an interview with President John Quincy Adams. It is said that the President did not want to do an interview with her, but Anne Royall soon learned that the President liked to skinny-dip in the Potomac at dawn. She hid and waited for the President to come along and strip down to his birthday suit. She waited until he was up to his neck in Potomac waters, then came out of hiding. Then she calmly proceeded to ask the President

questions for her interview, all the while sitting on the President's clothes. I'm sure the inception of the Secret Service came pretty close after that interview.

There was little we could do with our boat at this point along the river, so we returned by car on another day and walked around. As we stood by the Lincoln Memorial and looked straight across Memorial Bridge and up the hill, we saw Arlington House, home of Robert E. Lee and his wife, Mary Curtis. Mrs. Lee was the daughter of George Washington Parke Curtis, owner of the 1,100-acre Arlington estate and he willed it over to Mary upon his death. While staring up at the house, we saw a small fire burning in front of it; The Eternal Flame, gravesite of President John F. Kennedy. Buried with him are his two infant children. His widow lighted the flame in ceremonies three days after his assassination. Next to the 35th President of the United States lies his brother, Senator Robert F. Kennedy. According to an Arlington Cemetery brochure, the Kennedy gravesite is the most visited gravesite in the United States. The only other U.S. President buried in Arlington is William Howard Taft.

I noticed Tom and I spoke very little to each other while we were here; as if we were in church or afraid to disturb anything. We were surrounded by memorials - the Tomb of the Unknowns; the mast from the USS MAINE whose shadow passes over the final resting place of 229 sailors; the U.S. Coast Guard Monument; the Nurses Memorial; the memorial to the seven astronauts who lost their lives in the Space Shuttle Challenger accident, a memorial to those who lost their lives in the failed Iranian hostage rescue mission. Around us were

Memorials Along the Potomac — Arlington Memorial Bridge and Lincoln Memorial

the remains of people such as Joe Louis, the Heavyweight Boxing Champion; Admiral Hyman Rickover, Father of our Nuclear Navy; Abner Doubleday; Colonel "Pappy" Boyington of the USMC's Black Sheep squadron; Frank Reynolds, newscaster for ABC News; Audie Murphy, WWII's most decorated soldier; Navy Seabee Robert Stethem who was murdered by terrorists on a TWA aircraft in 1985; 21 Marines who lost their lives in the bombing of the Marine Compound in Beirut in 1983; and John Wesley Powell, the first person to explore the Grand Canyon. The list could not be complete without mentioning every gravestone, from Army Private to 5-star General, from Seaman to Admiral. Over 200,000 sailors, airmen and soldiers lie at rest on these hallowed grounds.

While we were there, I silently walked over to photograph the gravestone of a friend of mine, and then, feeling as one does when they extend their welcome, hurriedly left. We walked across Memorial Bridge and saw the Washington monument looming up behind the Lincoln Memorial. The Washington Monument is the tallest masonry structure in the world at 555 feet. The monument was dedicated in 1885 to the memory of the first United States president, George Washington.

The Lincoln Memorial itself is another awe-inspiring structure, with Lincoln sitting as designed by Daniel Chester French (the same design that appears on the reverse of the U.S. penny. For trivia fans, the U.S. penny is the only U.S. coin in which the same person appears on both sides of the coin). The words to Lincoln's Gettysburg Address and his 2nd Inaugural Address are etched in stone on either side of him.

The Lincoln Memorial is a classic Greek Temple that reminds one of the Parthenon on Acropolis in Athens. Around the memorial are 36 Doric columns, each one representing one of the 36 states that existed when Lincoln died. Yet surrounded by all the huge monuments built in honor to the likes of Washington, Lincoln and Jefferson, is a small monument in the shadow of the Lincoln Memorial. The monument honors John Ericcson, the inventor who designed and perfected the screw propeller, and thus, like James Rumsey and steam navigation, revolutionized the maritime industry. Ericcson also designed the ironclad Union ship, the MONITOR. That ship was engaged in the famous Civil War naval battle with the MERRIMAC in 1862 that changed naval warfare for all time.

Back in our boat, we floated by an interesting statue of seagulls on the Virginia side of the Potomac in front of the Lyndon Baines Johnson Grove. The grove sits on Columbia Island under the silent watch of the Pentagon. The Pentagon is the largest Government office building in the world at 3.7 million square feet. The statue is a memorial designed by sculptor Ernesto Bagni del Piatta in 1922, dedicated to all Americans who lost their lives at sea. It is called the Navy and Marine Memorial.

Looking back across the river we saw the Jefferson Memorial which honors the author of the Declaration of Independence and the Bill of Rights. The Jefferson Memorial is on the south side of the Tidal Basin. The Tidal Basin, filled with Potomac water, is surrounded by hundreds of Yoshino and Akebono cherry trees. The Tidal Basin is the site for the famous cherry blossoms that bloom in late March or early April every year. The trees were a gift from the Japanese in 1912, when Mrs. William Howard Taft expressed an interest in such trees. Although some trees were destroyed by random acts of violence during World War II, the parent trees in Tokyo faired much worse from neglect and bombings during the war. By 1952, relations between Japan and the United States had improved enough to where the National Capital Parks sent cuttings from the cherry trees in Washington to replenish the parent trees in Tokyo.

The Tidal Basin was designed by the Army Corps of Engineers to permit the incoming tide to enter the basin at the southwest gate (the gate facing the Potomac) and to remain there until high tide. As the tidal waters flowed

Enjoying the Potomac — Tidal Basin Painting of the Washington Monument with Cherry Blossoms in Full Bloom.

back down the Potomac, the ebb current of "stored water" in the Tidal basin also flowed back downstream, but flowed out through the southeast gate. The water went into the Washington Channel between Hains Point and Fort McNair. The Tidal Basin was built to flush the stagnant water out of the Washington Channel.

We continued to drift with the river, and we passed under a series of bridges on which Interstate 395 and the Metro subway cross the Potomac. Locally it is called the 14th Street Bridge. Those that have never crossed over the bridge but think that it sounds familiar may remember the cold January day in 1982 when an Air Florida jetliner took off from Reagan National Airport with too much ice on its wings and stalled. On its way down it crushed some cars on the bridge and knocked off part of the bridge railing before crashing into the Potomac. Very few survived.

We drifted under the 14th Street Bridge and the George Mason Memorial Bridge and around the tip of Hains Point, or East Potomac Park. Three separate flows of water merge at the southern end of Hains Point into the Potomac: the Anacostia River, once called the Eastern Branch of the Potomac; the Washington Channel, where many yachts, yacht clubs and marinas are located; and the Potomac River. An interesting sight along the Washington Channel is the Titanic Memorial. The memorial is visually impressive when you stand in front of it. The words on the monument read:

"To the brave men
who perished
in the wreck of the Titanic
April 15 1912.

They gave their
lives that women
and children
might be saved.
Erected by the
Women of America."

Across from the Washington Channel is Hains Point. The most amazing thing about Hains Point was the 5-piece set of giant sculptures entitled "The Awakening" that depicts a person rising up out of the ground. The first time I drove around the perimeter of Hains Point, I never realized that this sculpture was there and it startled me. I have seen it often since then, but by far the best time to see something that stark is when light fog rolls in. Tom and I went there on a cold winter day when few people were out enjoying the site. Recently the sculpture was relocated to the newly built National Harbor in Prince Georges County, Maryland, just south of the newly refurbished Woodrow Wilson Bridge.

The sculptor was commissioned to produce something that commemorated the rebirth, or awakening, of the Potomac. As it turned out, the middle 1960s almost killed the river. There was so much industrial and sewage waste being dumped into the river that the stench during the summer was unbearable. Warnings went out to fishermen not to eat anything that had been caught in the river. President Lyndon Baines Johnson was one who couldn't stand the stench of the river and he ordered the Government to do whatever they had to do to clean it up. That clean-up included the commissioning of "The Awakening."

Sculpture On the Potomac — "The Awakening"

Probably the only other person besides Major Pierre Charles L'Enfant (the person who designed the District of Columbia) who understood the relation that the city of Washington should have with the Potomac was General Hains from the Corps of Engineers. Hains built the point and on any summer Saturday or Sunday, people mob Hains Point. It probably provides as much enjoyment for the Washington area people as Central Park does for New Yorkers.

On the river at night is an experience one is not soon to forget. In our case, we were staring into the darkness off Hains Point and caught a glimpse of some lights moving on the water. The two red lights with a white light between them, or red-white-red, indicated a tug restricted in its ability to maneuver. As the distance between the tug and our boat decreased, the silhouette of a tugboat loomed in front of us. We saw that it was pushing a barge up into the Anacostia

River. It passed us and slowly drifted back into the darkness. We never got close enough to where we could read the name of the tug, but Tom and I laughed to think that this tugboat was "Cap't Tom." The tugboat "Cap't Tom" appears as a painting in this book and was a boat Tom and I continuously came across during our times on the river.

The Potomac that flows down the Virginia side splits around Columbia Island, home to the Columbia Island Marina. The 13-foot clearance under the fixed bridge eliminates just about everything but daysailers and small powerboats from entering this lagoon. By car and on foot, though, the area is delightful, surrounded by the white pines in the Lyndon B. Johnson Park. The marina has a newly refurbished dockmaster office and cafeteria with plenty of outside picnic tables to relax and enjoy the scenery.

At daybreak we motored over to a park just north of the Washington National Airport. Accessible only from the northbound lanes of the George Washington Memorial Parkway, it is a favorite place for a game of soccer or for watching the loud and low-flying aircraft on final approach land at the airport. Some even combine the two events and kick their soccer balls as high as they can when a plane flies overhead. The exhaust from the jet engines tosses the soccer ball around in sporadic jerks. Between the park and National Airport is a small but deep stream where a free boat ramp is located. If you continued inward along this stream and under the Parkway you would find yourself in Roaches Run. You also would find yourself hard aground, as this is a tidal lagoon. Since

you really shouldn't walk across the Parkway, it is best if you pulled into the parking lot just before the National Airport entrance ramp on the southbound side of the parkway. From fall to spring, dabbling ducks, black-crowned night herons and a variety of gulls show up on this lagoon.

While Washington National Airport is now the most desired airport for people who fly into the area, it was once one of many airfields in the area. One airfield was at the Anacostia Naval Base and another airfield was at Bolling Air Force Base.

The beginnings of both the Anacostia Naval Base and the Bolling Air Force Base on the east side of the Potomac just south of Anacostia River were simple. In a letter written in 1917 from the Chief of Army Engineers, Brigadier General W. M. Black, to the Chief Signal Officer of the Army, Brigadier General Black said "Referring to your letter of the 15th . . . authorizing you to occupy and use as an airplane site during the period November 1, 1917, and ending six months after the termination of the war, the area of Anacostia Flats in the District of Columbia..." With this, an airfield was formed.

Two days later, the Secretary of War wrote the Secretary of the Navy authorizing the Navy to use the area on the Anacostia Flats for "the erection and maintenance of a seaplane hangar; it being understood that the Army may have joint use of such land and water front at any time." The initial allocation for the building off the airfield was $500. An additional $30,000 was authorized for the construction of two hangars, two runways, a small office building and a barracks large enough to house and feed 100 men. The field was inaugurated on 1 January 1919.

It was at this base that Colonel Charles Lindbergh's *Spirit of Saint Louis*, now hanging at the Smithsonian's National Air and Space Museum, was unloaded from the hold of USS MEMPHIS. The plane was brought back across the Atlantic Ocean from France after Lindbergh's historic first solo flight across the Atlantic.

It was also here that the birth of the Navy's current aerial demonstration team, the Blue Angels, took place. During the early 1930s, Lieutenant Mathias B. Gardner, Lieutenant (junior grade) Aaron P. Stores and a Lieutenant (junior grade) Trapnell formed the Flying Fish - the earliest U.S. military flight demonstration team on record. Flying specially equipped Curtiss Hawks; they executed aerial maneuvers while flying with their wing tips connected to each other's plane by short lengths of cord.

Anacostia was home to the birth of formal aircraft testing, aerial photography, radio and broadcasting research. Many altitude and endurance records in land-based aircraft and seaplanes were broken here.

There was a good reason for this area to be called Anacostia Flats. During the early years of Anacostia and Bolling, four floods hit the airfields. Two of the most serious occurred during the spring seasons of 1936 and 1937, destroying records and machinery and inundating the buildings with silt and mud. Shortly afterward, a series of retaining walls were built along the Potomac River, which ended the problem of flooding river waters. It created another problem, though. During the heavy flooding of Hurricane Connie in 1954 and Hurricane

Agnes in 1972, the retaining walls also kept the waters inside, like a bathtub. These retaining walls can still be seen along the perimeter where the waters of the Potomac press against the two military bases.

Between July 1 and July 15, 1943, the Navy's Flight Test Department, Radio Test Department and Aircraft Experiment and Development Squadron left Anacostia and moved to Naval Air Station Patuxent River, Maryland. Those units became the predecessors of today's Patuxent River Naval Air Test Center.

The congestion in the airspace surrounding the three airfields, Naval Air Station Anacostia, Bolling Air Force Base and National Airport, was growing into a serious problem. A joke at the air bases was that a pilot approaching Anacostia needed to have three eyes - One to watch his gauges, one to watch his approach, and one to watch out for all the other air traffic in the area.

Another problem that sounded the death knell for the bases as airfields was the arrival of the first jets. It was in 1957 that the stations received their first jet— the TV-2 trainer. Many senior VIPs witnessed the first landing of this jet at Anacostia. They all watched in horror as the plane came in on final approach, touched down, and took the entire length of the runway to stop. The runways could not be lengthened without building them out into the Potomac and Anacostia Rivers.

Because of airspace congestion with National Airport and the runway length required for jet aircraft, the Department of Defense issued a statement in April 1958 that the bases would be closed by 1962. The Naval Air Station Anacostia and Bolling Air Force Base would both move to nearby Andrews Air Force Base.

The last jet to fly out of Anacostia was a Douglas A4 D Skyhawk on January 25, 1961. The plane had come to Washington to participate in the inauguration of President John F. Kennedy.

Today the military bases are home to units like the Navy's Audio-Visual Center (formerly and better known as the Naval Photographic Center), staging area for the President's HMX-1 helicopter squadron (headquartered at Quantico Marine Air Station further south along the Potomac), the Defense Intelligence Agency, and, further south, the Naval Research Lab.

We had now motored past National Airport and were south of the main runway when we tried to locate the Four Mile Run stream that flows into the Potomac between the Washington Marina (Patowmack Landing) and the south side of National Airport. At the mouth of this stream can be seen ruddy ducks, green-winged teal, horned grebes and diving ducks.

Power on the Potomac

From a shallow-hulled boat, we hugged the shoreline south of Washington Marina and inched our way up among the sailboats and sailboarders. At the last buoy on our right, we pulled around and headed toward National Airport to watch the birds and the water trickling into the Potomac. For those driving cars, pull into and park at the Washington Marina and walk north toward the airport on the bike path until you reach the cove. At the northern end of the cove is the end of Four Mile Run.

Our first stab at entering the Marina by boat resulted in running aground in low tide - in a Chris-Craft no less. A few feet away, deeper-draft sailboats went by on their merry way. So much for maintaining the right-of-way. So we figured we would just relax, pretend we knew what we were doing, and just shoot pictures of the sailboats and the marina while the tide came in. Then we realized that the tide was indeed coming in, from the south naturally, and pushing us a little farther up into the mud as time went by. So we walked up to the bow and with our combined weight effectively pulled the boat propeller up and out of the mud in the rear of the boat. With much churning mud, the captain backed out. For some reason, I have many pictures of aircraft taking off from National Airport that day. With National Airport behind us, our next goal was Old Town Alexandria.

In our quest to obtain a panoramic view of Old Town, we sailed over to the eastern side of the Potomac, just north of the Woodrow Wilson Bridge. To get there we had to fight our way through the ever-increasing clumps of hydrilla. Hydrilla is a rapidly growing plant that is becoming the scourge of the river as it chokes the entrance to smaller creeks, reduces the flow of the river, forces the closure of some marinas, and becomes, simply, a downright pest. There are advocates of the plant, of course, who claim the plant acts as a filter for the river and is making the river a cleaner place to fish in. It is also said that the hydrilla also gives safe haven for the newly born fish and a better chance for them to survive. Fishermen claim that the biggest "lunkers," better known to those that don't fish as "big fish," hang around right at the edge of these islands of hydrilla. What I fear is happening is that in a few years from now, the hydrilla will have caught enough debris and soil moving down the river that these beds of hydrilla will eventually become solid islands themselves.

We passed through the hydrilla and found to our surprise an area of beach that seemed to collect every bit of refuse that washes down the Potomac. This area is a veritable archeological dig for those who want to see how people live and what they throw away. We found that the quiet tree-lined river is also a conduit for our trash. We found a few sun-bleached tree trunks and other natural driftwood lying on the beach. For the most part, though, we were awed by the waste we saw, including hundreds of car tires, many embedded in the sand while other were resting comfortably on top of the sand, only recently having their found their way to the equivalent of an elephant burial ground for old tires. Baby buggies, tennis balls, wooden boxes, plastic of all kinds, dead rats and the list goes on, were littered across the beach. In a way, these tires must help keep the beach from washing away, a tolerant coexistence. It was so appalling, so out of the ordinary from the beautiful Potomac scenes we had witnessed in our travels that Tom captured the scene with watercolor and brush. We experienced many aspects of the river, but none portrayed the river's fragile existence as clearly as "Tire Beach."

William Presley, the first representative to qualify for a seat in the Virginia House of Burgesses in 1647, was the author of the Potomac's first protective ordinance: "There shall be no man or woman, Launderer or Laundress, dare to wash any unclean Linnen, drive bucks, or throwe out the water of suds of fowle clothes in the open stretts within the Pallizadoes, or within forty feet of the same, not rench .. any kettle, pot or pan ... within twenty foote of the olde well, or new Pumpe, nor shall anyone aforesaid, within one quarter of one mile ... doe the necessities of nature, since by these unmanly, slothful, and loathsome immodesties the whole Fort may be choked and poisoned by ill airs." The Washington Post issue dated December 30, 1973, stated that the Washington, D.C., metropolitan area was dumping 404,000,000 gallons of untreated sewage into the Potomac River every day.

We crossed the Potomac and snuggled up along the piers of the Old Dominion Yacht Club in Old Town Alexandria. Having missed a good part of the Alexandria waterfront, we worked our way back upstream, pointing the bow of our boat toward the PEPCO power plant. The history of Alexandria goes back nearly as far as the discovery of the Potomac itself

The Polluted Potomac — Tire Beach

by Captain John Smith. It started in the 1740's with the establishment of tobacco warehouses. The tobacco industry prospered and so did the little settlement that had grown up around the warehouses. Seven years after the warehouses were built, John West, Jr., and his young assistant, George Washington, surveyed the settlement and, according to the history books, "laid off in streets and 84 half-acre lots" the town of Alexandria. Having surveyed Alexandria, the next thing to do was to sell the half-acre lots. On an early morning in July, 1749, the lots were offered for public sale and some of the first buyers were such notables as William Fairfax, Lawrence and Augustus Washington, and John Carlyle. Alexandria later became the hometown of George Mason, Robert E. Lee, and George Washington himself.

During the Civil War, Alexandria was protected from the Confederates who were marching north toward the capitol. Alexandria was surrounded by Federal troops bent on protecting the navigable Potomac River around Alexandria.

In 1789, Alexandria was ceded to the District of Columbia, but after the Civil War, the Southern-dominated Alexandrians petitioned Congress to return Alexandria to the Old Dominion, and Congress agreed. Alexandria declined as a center of commerce until around 1914 when the Alexandria shipyards were reopened and the Naval Torpedo Factory was built. Today Alexandria has developed back into a commercial and transportation center and the Naval Torpedo Factory is now home to some 175 professional artists of various media.

We reached the Virginia shoreline between Marina Towers and the piles of coal at the PEPCO plant and then turned downstream. As we huddled close to the Alexandria shoreline, we came across a lock that looked just like those locks on the C&O Canal. If this one was open we could have motored in from the Potomac River itself. It was the Tide Lock of the Alexandria Canal.

Next to the Tide Lock were three items oddly out of sequence with the surroundings: two huge eyes staring at us from atop a wall, a miniature version of the Washington Monument, and a pair of huge marble lips spitting water. This was too much to pass up and we tied our boat to a rock along the jetty and climbed ashore. We were almost hit by the skateboarders using the twists and turns of the sidewalk to do their acrobatics. An old man was fishing off the rocks close to where our boat was, so we left to figure out what these ruins of a Greek amphitheater was doing along the shoreline. We had come face to face with a sculpturer's rendition of the last days of Pompeii and we soon discovered ourselves at the TransPotomac Canal Center. After wandering back to check out the lock, we soon came across a very pleasant surprise: The Alexandria Waterfront Museum. It was early Sunday afternoon, but we tried the door anyway. It was unlocked. What we entered was more than just another museum to help develop a waterfront. What we found was a very serious and determined museum struggling to get itself established as a research center for the history, development and social life of the Alexandria waterfront. The waterfront included the Alexandria Canal. Its research department holds archives of canal books, slides and prints for the serious student.

The Alexandria Waterfront Museum is owned and operated by the City of Alexandria and, as we soon found out, is located next to the Tide Lock of the Alexandria Canal. This canal, like the better known C&O Canal, was a business venture to take advantage of the C&O Canal by hooking up to it with an aqueduct at the present day Key Bridge connecting Rosslyn, Virginia, to Georgetown in Washington, D.C. You can still see the remnants of the aqueduct to the left of the boathouse that is on the upstream side of Key Bridge on the Washington side. After the Civil War, the Alexandria Canal fell into disuse and people soon began tossing their trash into it. This was good news for the Alexandria archaeologists who discovered that even the local glass factory was tossing their trash into the canal. It didn't take many years before the canal was covered completely over. If you watch the museum's 14-minute film on the excavation of the Tide Lock, you'll learn that the Tide Lock walls were 7 to 14 feet underground when they excavated enough to find them.

We walked around the canal, crossed over a replica of the original Tide Lock Bridge, past the spitting lips and replica of the Washington Monument again, and went back to our boat to continue our downstream journey.

Further down we passed the Virginia Schools Rowing Facility where high school students were getting ready to learn the fine art of crewing from an instructor with the Virginia Public School system. After passing them, we swung into Oronico Bay and saw a brownish building in front of us that marked itself as the focus point for this area. Tom and I agreed that it looked the same to both of us: like the superstructure of a futuristic aircraft carrier. It is called the Edward F. Carlough Plaza, but it is really the Headquarters of the Sheet Metal Workers National Pension Fund. In

front of the building, and wrapping itself around the edge of the Oronico Bay, was Oronico Bay Park. The word "oronico" is Indian for "a place to paddle" or "a navigable place." The picnic tables were deserted except one under a tree where a large family was enjoying the sunny and breezy afternoon. Although the adults were oblivious to it, we watched a small child at the picnic who had attracted seagulls by throwing pieces of his sandwich down on the ground. The number of gulls increased, and the sandwich disappeared into the growing mob scene. The child must have thought that the birds would leave when the sandwich was gone, but the gulls remained and grew noisy. They began fighting over smaller pieces of the sandwich that were overlooked in favor of the larger pieces. With no more food and the gulls growing restless and fighting, it became a scene right out of Alfred Hitchcock's The Birds. The child panicked and ran back to the picnic table.

Leaving the bay, we rounded a warehouse called Robinson Terminal Warehouse North and passed a small park called Founders Park. We then came across a small white building sitting on the dock with the sign "DOCKMASTER" on it. Then we came across a more familiar site known as The Torpedo Factory. Once home to the U.S. Navy's Submarine Torpedo plant, it has now been turned into a community of artists with some 175 shops. In the small harbor at The Torpedo Factory a small boat called ADMIRAL TILP was providing tourists with a tour of the Alexandria waterfront. The boat was named for Frederick Tilp, a person whose love for the Potomac River prompted him to self-publish an endearing book on the river in 1978 called *This Was Potomac River* and who became known as the expert on any matters about the Potomac. The press sought him out for any quotation concerning the Potomac River.

Past The Torpedo Factory we drew in close to the shore and bumped up against the seawall of the Alexandria Waterfront Park. Ahead of us was a 3-masted wooden sailing ship, a "Tall Ship," tied to a pier and open for free tours. The ship is a permanent attraction to draw tourists to Old Town and is named, appropriately, ALEXANDRIA. Nearby, a group of visitors in another boat was celebrating a birthday and a bottle of champagne was popped open. We pushed away from the seawall, rounded the Alexandria, and immediately came across another boat. This one was a glass-enclosed boat whose single-minded purpose was far removed from the 3-masted sailing ships of yesterday. This ship was the DANDY and its purpose

is to take people out on cruises up and down the river and to provide food, drink, and music for dancing.

We passed DANDY and saw the buildings housing Potomac Arms and Interarms, both clearinghouses for gun shipments coming into and leaving the area, mostly by boat. Interarms is considered the world's largest private arms dealer. Then we motored past Robinson Terminal Warehouse South. About once a week a freighter arrives at the terminal and drops off a huge amount of goods, including newsprint paper. The paper is stored at the warehouse and then moved to plants around the area where it is used for the daily newspapers.

Finishing our tour of the area, we passed Roberdeau Park, Pommander Park, and almost reached the seawall of the Jones Point National Park, where dozens of people were casting their fishing lines into the river.

CHAPTER 5

From the Woodrow Wilson Bridge to Smith Point Lighthouse

We motored past the Jones Point National Park in Old Town Alexandria, located where the Woodrow Wilson Bridge touches the Virginia shore. We motored up to a white building at the most southern tip of Jones Point that looked like an old lighthouse. The building is protected by the Mount Vernon Chapter of the Daughters of the American Revolution because of its historical significance. On September 6, 1654, this site was included in a patent of 700 acres granted by the Colony of Virginia to Mistress Margaret Brent. Mistress Brent was a woman who spent most of her adult life fighting discrimination of her sex. She was the first private owner of this rectangular tract of land that became the nucleus of Alexandria.

We walked around the house and at the foot of the stairs we came upon a block of stone about three feet square. The stone had a hole about six inches in diameter drilled through the middle of it. We looked down the hole and saw another square block of stone, with a corner of that stone centered below the hole of the stone above it. This stone, also protected by the Mount Vernon Chapter of the Daughters of the American Revolution, was the original Federal Boundary Stone for the District of Columbia that was placed here on April 15, 1791.

When the District of Columbia was designed, the area was going to be 100 square miles; 10 miles on each side of a square. Each corner of the square points due north, east, west, and south, like a diamond on a playing card. Those 100 square miles encompassed land from Maryland and Virginia, and the area taken up by the Potomac River and its tributaries. This surveyor's stone was proof that we were standing at the southernmost point of Washington, D.C. With Congress having given back to Virginia the District land west of the Potomac, the District of Columbia is comprised now of only 67 of its original 100 square miles. It is interesting that the legal documents that formed the 100 square miles for the District of Columbia never mentioned transferring the rights of the Potomac to D.C. It could be assumed that Maryland still legally owns the Potomac now claimed by the District.

Another argument could be that Virginia and West Virginia could lay claim to half the Potomac. The nautical term for this ownership is 'thalweg' which means 'the line of deepest sounding.' The line of deepest sounding is usually in the middle of the body of water. This means that the ownership of a body of water between two states is split at the deepest part of the body of water. For example, the state boundary between Maryland and Virginia along Maryland's Eastern Shore starting at the mouth of the Chesapeake Bay is at the thalweg of the Pocomoke River. The thalweg then zigzags westward up to Smith Point, Virginia, at the mouth of the Potomac River. Suddenly the boundary line formula changes from 'thalweg' to 'at the high water mark' along Virginia's shore of the Potomac, thus giving Maryland all the Potomac. So why doesn't Virginia and West Virginia own half the Potomac? It goes back to when Virginia expelled the Quakers from the Virginia Colony.

In 1660, an Act of the Virginia Assembly, expelling the Quakers from that colony, under severe penalties, compelled the Quakers to seek a new home and refuge in Maryland. The persecuted Quakers of the Eastern shore of Virginia petitioned Governor Calvert to afford them facilities for settling in Maryland, and in compliance with their petition, in November, 1661, he granted lands on the Eastern shore of Maryland to those Virginians who wished to come with their families into Maryland.

Unfortunately, the Eastern shores belonging to Maryland and Virginia appeared to overlap and Virginia insisted that severe penalties should still be administered to those Quakers that had moved, as they appeared not to have moved out of Virginia. Unprovoked hostilities by Virginians attempting to move the Quakers further away prompted the Governor of Maryland to begin negotiations with Berkeley, the Governor of Virginia. They appointed a commission on the June 25, 1668, to mark and agree upon the boundary line between the two states running all the way to the ocean. While an agreement came out of that commission, the sovereignty of the Potomac River remained unsettled until a century after the American Revolution. Finally, Maryland and Virginia consented to submit their claims to a board of arbitrators to ascertain and determine the true line of the boundary. After examining a vast amount of evidence, historical, documentary and oral, hearing elaborate arguments of counsel on both sides, and conferring fully on the merits and demerits of this ancient controversy, the arbitrators, in January, 1877, came to a final decision, subject to ratification of the two States and Congress. It is a long and interesting report on the boundary lines, and the sum of their conclusions as concerns the Potomac River was: "The low-water mark on the Potomac, to which Virginia has a right in the soil, is to be measured from low-water mark at one headland to one low-water mark at another, without following indentations, bays, creeks, inlets or affluent rivers. Virginia is entitled not only to full dominion over the soil to low-water mark on the south shore of the Potomac, but has a right to such use of the river beyond the line of low-water mark as may be necessary or otherwise interfering with the proper use of it by Maryland, agreeably to the compact of 1785." By a decision of the majority, Maryland was awarded sovereignty over the whole of the Potomac River to its southern bank, except that Virginia was to have dominion over the soil to the low-water mark on the south side of the river. It is interesting to note that West Virginia never participated through direct response or through arbitrators as to how this decision would affect the Potomac along their boundary, having broken off from Virginia during the Civil War. The arbitrators never included West Virginia in the Potomac dispute. Nevertheless, the ownership of the Potomac River and the North Branch of the Potomac all the way back to Kempton, Maryland, belongs to Maryland.

Back in our boat, we headed over to the Maryland shoreline just south of the Woodrow Wilson Bridge at Oxon Hill and Smoots Cove, located in Prince George's County. Smoots Cove is a circular cove formed by a natural underwater spring. It has become a haven for sailboats as the current keeps the hydrilla out from the cove; it is also a favorite fishing spot.

The cars parked along Interstate 95 (the Capitol Beltway) on the Maryland side of the Woodrow Wilson Bridge are a good indication of the number of people fishing along the banks of the Potomac River near Smoots Cove. There used to be a semi-submerged hulk in Smoots Cove that resembled the rounded hull of a submarine. U.S. Navy divers, before pulling up their figurative anchor on their Navy Yard headquarters and moving to Panama City, Florida, used to train on this hulk.

Smoots Cove is also home to thousands of crushed firearms. The massive collection of illegal firearms and "Saturday night specials" are crushed for some local police departments and deposited into the deep waters here. Anyone with a strong magnet on the end of a fishing line can recover some of these arms. Some people have, but the arms are so badly mangled that they cannot be repaired.

Oxon Hill's claim to fame could be that it lost the body of a president of the United States. Yes, physically lost.

He was John Hanson of Maryland. Hanson was Chairman of the Maryland delegation to the Continental Congress when the Articles of Confederation were approved in 1781. He was elected president of the United States by the Congress under the terms of the document that had just been put into effect. Hanson served a one-year term as president in 1781-82. Hanson preceded George Washington by eight years. George Washington was elected president under the terms of the new Constitution in 1789.

In 1783 Hanson became ill and traveled to the home of his nephew in Oxon Hill. There he died and, presumably, was buried on the estate. There is no marker, headstone or any other indication of where the body of the first president of the United States lies buried. While many believe that George Washington was the first president of the United States, he was the eighth, but the first under the terms of the new Constitution.

John Hanson is the only president of the United States whose remains are lost. The site where other U.S. presidents are buried have become well known shrines. George Washington is buried at Mount Vernon, Abraham Lincoln is in Springfield, Illinois, Woodrow Wilson is interred in the Washington National Cathedral, John F. Kennedy's Eternal Flame is burning in the quiet of Arlington National Cemetery, and Harry Truman is in Independence, Missouri. Other presidents are buried in simple gravesites, but at least they can be located. Unfortunately, the last resting place of the first president of the United States elected "in Congress assembled" is not known and is somewhere in Oxon Hill.

Oxon Hill appears to have been named from the estate of "Oxon Hill manor" built in 1685 by Colonel John Addison, a privy counselor of Lord Baltimore. The Addison family had close ties with Oxford, England, and Oxoniensis is Latin for "of Oxford."

We motored downstream from the Woodrow Wilson Bridge and around Rosier Bluff to escape the hydrilla. Then we headed back across to the Virginia shore, pointing the boat toward Dyke Marsh.

Along the Belle Haven Picnic Area and Marina just south of Alexandria, besides the George Washington Memorial Parkway heading to Mount Vernon, is Dyke Marsh. This freshwater marsh is a shallow area with a tidal range of 3 feet. It is a prime birding spot near Washington, D.C.; over 250 species have been counted. From spring through fall you can see yellow and blue wild iris, sunflowers, and rose mallows in the marsh.

The use of the inflatable was taking its toll on our knees, clothes, camera gear and us. We were convinced that we could conclude the Potomac trip by another means of transportation. We finished the day in the inflatable but later, in a friend's Chris-Craft, we visited Fort Washington, near the northern side of the mouth of Piscataway Creek. This fort was constructed to protect Washington, D.C., and is a good example of early 19th century fortifications. It lies low to the ground and you could easily miss it if it wasn't for the large white marker guarding the fort from the shoreline.

Not far from Accokeek at the southern side of the mouth of Piscataway Creek lies Piscataway Park, managed by the National Park Service primarily to protect the view from Mount Vernon across the Potomac. The Park Service owns 1,500 acres along the shore outright and holds scenic easements on some 3,000 acres of private residential lands on the surrounding hills. The complex includes the National Colonial Farm of the Accokeek Foundation and a demonstration of a late 18th Century farm typical of this region. It is also home to the Hard Bargain Farm (Ferguson Farm), operated by the Alice Ferguson

Foundation as an environmental study area for elementary school students. There are several trails for nature-minded hikers. Many emerge along the banks of the Potomac (Mockley Point and the Visitor's Center at Bryan Point) where one can view Mount Vernon through binoculars. Between these two points of land are the remains of the old Piscataway Indian burial grounds.

There was a Piscataway Indian settlement called Moyaone at the mouth of Piscataway Creek. The present Cedarville Natural Resources Management Area served as their winter camping ground because of its mild climate and abundant game. From the Potomac all we saw was a solid line of trees hugging the shore. Our next stop was more memorable: Mount Vernon.

Mount Vernon was, of course, the home of George Washington. Its name comes from Admiral Vernon, a British naval officer under whom George Washington's elder half-brother, Lawrence, served. Located in an area called "Little Reach," (that stretch of the Potomac between Whitestone Point and Fort Washington), there is a gazebo/dock just south of Mount Vernon. You can tie up to it for a short time while you unload any passengers, but the dockmaster wants you out of there when the larger cruiseboats come dieseling down from Washington or Alexandria with their tourists. Mount Vernon is one of the greatest historic places overlooking the Potomac and was painted by Tom. It is interesting to watch any U.S. Navy ship passing Mount Vernon.

U.S. Navy regulation Article 2185, enacted in 1948, states:

The Historic Potomac — Mount Vernon

"When a ship of the U.S. Navy is passing Washington's tomb at Mount Vernon, between sunrise and sunset, the following ceremonies shall be observed insofar as may be practical: the full guard and band shall be paraded, the bell tolled, and the national ensign half-masted at the beginning of the tolling of the bell. When opposite Washington's tomb, the guard shall present arms, persons on deck shall salute, facing in the direction of the tomb, and taps shall be sounded. The national ensign shall be two-blocked and the tolling shall cease at the last note of taps, after which the national anthem shall be played. Upon completion of the anthem, carry-on shall be sounded. The bell is struck eight times at five-second intervals. In the absence of a band, a whistle or bosun's pipe may be used."

The first account of such a ceremony being enacted was in May 1801 when the frigate USS CONGRESS sailed past Washington's tomb. All sails were lowered and 13 cannon fired as a salute. Cannon were used until shortly after the Civil War, when many local farmers petitioned to have it stopped as it was scaring their livestock.

The reason Mount Vernon exists in such pristine condition can be credited to Miss Ann Pamela Cunningham of South Carolina who, in 1853, founded the Mount Vernon Ladies' Association. This group, considered the oldest preservation organization in America, generated the financial support that permitted them to purchase the estate in 1858 from John Washington, Jr., George Washington's great-grand-nephew.

Mount Vernon and the Potomac had a direct influence on the writing of the United States Constitution. It began shortly after the American Revolution when problems arose concerning the navigational laws on the Potomac. Skirmishes erupted over whether Virginia or Maryland had any rights to make navigational laws for those who plied the Potomac. This led to a meeting of Commissioners from Maryland and Virginia in 1785 at Mount Vernon with George Washington chairing the meeting. This preliminary gathering led to a larger convention that met in Annapolis in 1786 to discuss interstate commercial problems, of which the Potomac played a part. Only a few states sent representatives, so Alexander Hamilton decided to call upon all the states to meet again in Philadelphia in 1787 to discuss

"all matters necessary to render the Constitution of the Federal Government adequate to the exigencies of the Union," which included interstate commercial problems. The Philadelphia Convention, better known as the Constitutional Convention, convened in May of 1787 and resulted in the writing of the United States Constitution.

As we cruised on the Potomac I had to check the charts twice before being convinced that what we were looking at was really Mount Vernon. I expected something more befitting a man of his stature. I was expecting something massive, a palace of sorts, an elegant mansion. What I saw was just someone's home. A home where a portion of trees had been felled so that an unobstructed view of the Potomac was possible from the back porch. It takes more than just looking at this home from the water to realize that, in its own way, it was massive.

A walk through the home and the surrounding grounds gives you the distinct impression that George didn't need a palace, just a farmhouse with pine floors and some mahogany furnishings to retire to. With the morning sun lighting up the eastern side of Mount Vernon, one sees vividly the eight square columns on the back porch with their shadows against the building and the red roof. You can easily imagine Washington at home in his garden. Past Mount Vernon, the Potomac reigns supreme. Upstream, the Potomac would at times become secondary to the sights of the Washington, D.C., monuments or to the massive rocks at Great Falls. Here, though, until the

Historic Potomac — Mount Vernon Boathouse

river flows into the Chesapeake, it is the widening and deepening Potomac that first draws one's attention.

We passed Ferry Point and Dogue Creek on the Virginia side. Dogue Creek, pronounced dawg, was named after an Indian tribe of Dogues, or Dawgs, who lived in this area and had the terrible reputation of being pure evil. The saying "mean as a dog" is a corruption from the colonial saying "mean as a dawg."

Tom and I passed the Fort Belvoir Officers' Club overlooking the Potomac. Colonel Fairfax established residence on this property and was the one who gave the area the name Belvoir, in honor of his ancestral home in England. The name means "beautiful to see."

Tom and I veered slightly into Gunston Cove to look at Gunston Hall. Further up Gunston Cove is Accotink Bay and Pohick Bay. The word 'pohick' is a shortened name for pohickory, which is Indian for a certain American tree, which we now call hickory. Tom and I weren't checking the area for hickory trees, though, but for the home of George Mason.

George Mason was another person, with George Washington, who would have rather tended his gardens at home than commute back and forth to Washington. While George Washington lived and worked from Mount Vernon, George Mason lived and worked a few miles south in another modest home along the Virginia shore overlooking the Potomac. George Mason's home was Gunston Hall. George Mason's claim to fame? Well, read this:

> "That all men are by nature equally free and independent, and have certain inherent rights, namely, the enjoyment of life and liberty ...."

That is from the Virginia Declaration of Rights that Mason wrote. Thomas Jefferson must have really liked the way that sounded since very similar wording appeared in our Constitution's Bill of Rights.

Mason designed the home himself sometime before 1755. The original paint colors have been restored in many rooms, and many pieces originally owned by Mason are among the furnishings, including the desk at which he wrote the Virginia Declaration of Rights.

The daily tours, the library research, and the road and water trips were pretty much concluded. With the inflatable boat now packed away for awhile, it was decided to finish the final portion of on-the-water research in style.

It was just after sunrise on what was to be another typically hot summer day when Tom and I met John Fisher and his Chris-Craft motorboat at the Woodbridge Marina.

George Mason owned Woodbridge, originally called Occoquan Plantation. George Mason's son Thomas named the area now called Woodbridge for the wooden bridge that was built across the Occoquan River in 1798, replacing the ferry.

We climbed aboard John's boat, released the lines, and John slipped the throttle a notch into reverse. Then the throttle slipped slightly forward as he edged our way out between other boats and into the Occoquan River. John was careful not to create a wake until well past the other boats nestled against their slips.

We passed Massey Creek on our left and moved into Belmont Bay, where John pushed the throttle forward. We motored past Conrad Island, John needling his way neatly between Deephole Point and Sandy Point, then crossed Occoquan Bay. Within minutes we found ourselves passing Freestone Point on our right in Virginia (which is part of the Mason Neck National Wildlife Refuge) and Cornwallis Neck on our left in Maryland. We were again on the Potomac River with a full day of exploration and surprises ahead of us. On the Maryland side was Potomac Heights and the Navy's Indian Head military base. The area was desolate before 1890 when the Navy moved its proving grounds here. For a time it was called the U.S. Naval Propellant Plant producing solid rocket fuel. It is now called the U.S. Naval Ordnance Station, covering 2,072 acres. Across Mattawoman Creek at Stump Neck is the Navy's Explosive Ordnance Disposal School, an annex of the Indian Head Plant, created in the 1940s.

Today was a red letter day; we would complete our Potomac journey moving downstream until we reached Smith Point Lighthouse in the Chesapeake Bay. Although Smith Point Lighthouse is in the Chesapeake Bay, Tom and I consider the lighthouse to be the official end of the Potomac River. The lighthouse is named after Smith Point, physically the southernmost point of the mouth of the Potomac River. Smith Point is named after John Smith who sailed up the Potomac and landed at Georgetown to trade with the Indians. Our goal today was very satisfying - to complete our journey that began at the Fairfax Stone in West Virginia. Along the way today we would again photograph what we called targets of opportunity - those interesting and picturesque scenes that I rarely found in my research but usually discovered by surprise in our travels. There were many targets found today. One was an old barn hanging over the cliff ready to topple into the Potomac because the river had slowly eroded the soil out from underneath it. Others were the rusted hulls of shipwrecks at various points along the Maryland shoreline.

Tom pointed out our position to me on Nautical Chart 12285, "POTOMAC RIVER: Washington D.C., Maryland, Virginia." While we passed Powells Creek on the Virginia side, we passed Mattawoman Creek on the Maryland side. We quickly adapted to the speed of the boat and to the sound of the Potomac water trying to pound its way through the bow.

We passed Chicamuxen Creek on the Maryland shore and then passed under the overhead power cables that stretched across the river 170 feet above us. We swung in close to hug the Virginia shoreline as we passed the PEPCO power plant. John cut back the engine as we watched an Amtrak train cross the fixed bridge at Quantico Creek. Quantico Creek brought back memories for me.

I spent one summer taking an underwater archeology course from Capital Divers Association. Don Shomette, a noted maritime writer and diver split the course in half with the first half consisting of eight weeks of night classes. The second half of the course was spent in Quantico Creek, working on a Civil War shipwreck near the PEPCO plant. Library research had showed that the remains of this shipwreck were the Confederate side-wheel steamer C.S.S. GEORGE PAGE. This vessel was a 410-ton river defense ship originally built and owned by the Union and captured by the Confederates at Aquila Creek, Virginia, in May 1861. What made this wreck interesting enough to SCUBA in muddy water and near zero visibility was that this was the only Confederate gunboat to operate on the Potomac River. After many measurements of what remained of the hull and some artifact recovery attempts, we began calling ourselves "Club Mud." We could never prove that it was the GEORGE PAGE or any other ship we had researched as being there in Quantico Creek. Our research did tell us that this area of Quantico Creek also was used as a dumping ground in the early 20th century for housing construction waste. We found that this shipwreck had accumulated scrap electrical wiring and fixtures, and even some porcelain bathroom fixtures. Somewhere in Quantico Creek, according to detailed historical records, is a boat whose claim to fame was that it was the only Confederate gunboat to operate on the Potomac. Historical records say the Confederates placed charges in the boat and blew the stern off to sink it; thus preventing it from falling back into the hands of the Union. It appeared that the wreck was missing its stern, but the material and manufacture of the portholes suggested a later built vessel. I was told that the two deck guns that comprised the ship's battery were retrieved and restored years ago and now are displayed outside the Prince William County's courthouse. Still, there was no confirmation that this was the vessel that the guns were removed from. Potomac tidal waters are still bathing the shipwreck we spent the summer measuring, drawing and partially excavating. Parts of its broken deck are still sticking up out of the water at low tide, now stripped of portholes.

Fresh water flowing down the Potomac meets salt water flowing up from the Chesapeake at Quantico. Here the current is usually about 1.5 to 2 knots and the ebb current slowly and methodically pulls everything downstream. The current, of course, slows when the salt water from the Chesapeake begins flowing upstream as high tide approaches.

We passed the town of Quantico, which is an Indian word meaning "dancing" or "place of dancing." Today it is a quiet town surrounded by the U.S. Marine Corps base whose economy is based on little more than what the Marines spend. If you want to visit the town of Quantico, you may do so by boat or by first entering the Marine base. It is a symbiotic relationship. This is the closest "civilian" place for Marines to reach from their barracks. In return, the town caters to the Marines with barber shops, restaurants bedecked in Marine Corps paraphernalia, a bookstore with a large military section, and other miscellaneous shops. The Quantico Marina in town is operated by the Marine Corps, and

is a great place for military families to rent a sailboat or motorboat for a day on the Potomac.

Our next stop was at Chopawamsic Island, nestled alongside the Quantico Marine base. The island lies at the mouth of Chopawamsic Creek. The Indian name is an Algonquian sentence meaning, roughly, "They go down to the river." While we had originally planned to make this a photo opportunity, we did not plan to stay as long as we did. What we found as we drifted near the island were a couple of homes still being lived in, and a very photogenic rusted-out jeep sitting on a barge tethered to the island. This is a privately-owned island and there is no bridge connecting the island to the mainland. We were held near the island longer than anticipated by a large bed of hydrilla. We had succeeded in wrapping a dozen or so of these plants around our propeller. We swung the engine up and Tom leaned over the boat railing and yanked hunks of this green hydrilla off from around the propeller. John started the engine again, engaged the propeller and slowly skirted around some more beds. We moved into deeper water and headed across the river to another very interesting sight - Mallows Bay.

Mallows Bay used to be called Marlow's Bay, but the name was changed because of the abundance of a certain flower that was growing all over the shallow bay - the marsh mallow. While it may seem incredulous, you would be correct if you thought that marsh mallows had something to do with marshmallows. If you've ever eaten a real marshmallow, you may have eaten something made using the starchy root of the marsh mallow!

The real story about Mallows Bay has nothing to do with marshmallows but with shipwrecks—lots of them.

It was President Woodrow Wilson who, having been informed of the need for more ships during World War I, created the Emergency Fleet Corporation. Initial plans called for a fleet of some 1,000 wooden ships to be built in 18 months; later, the number contracted for would only reach 731. Bureaucracy and mismanagement reared their ugly heads, and of the 731 ships contracted for, only 98 were delivered before the end of the war. Even with the end of war, and after a Congressional investigation, the Emergency Fleet Corporation continued to build and deliver these

Bridges across the Potomac — The Route 301 Bridge

wooden boats. Eventually, 285 leaking vessels were tied up at piers along the Pacific and Atlantic coasts. Often, the Government was charged pumping and tug fees to keep the boats afloat. It seems that the boats were built with freshly sawn timber, and when the timber shrunk it left many holes in these ships.

Finally, 212 of these ships were sold to the Western Marine and Salvage Company of Alexandria. This company was formed for the specific purpose of purchasing these boats and stripping them of their scrap metal content. The ships were burned down to their waterlines at Widewater, Virginia, directly across from us as we drifted around Mallows Bay. After burning, they were tied together and towed over to the Maryland shoreline for some additional stripping and then abandoned to rot. They did not rot away as many expected. Instead, they have almost become an extension of the shoreline itself. Some now stick up out of the water with trees and flowers growing out from them. They have also become havens for fish, which in turn attracted the birds (there are even some bald eagle nests in the area). We even saw a wrecked houseboat up along the shore. The houseboat looked vaguely familiar to both Tom and I. It wasn't until I went back to reread the late Frederick Tilp's book "That Was The Potomac" that I saw it again. The houseboat we saw looked like a floating brothel that floated in the Potomac off the Port of Alexandria back in the days when tall-masted wooden ships would pull in to have their cargo unloaded. Tilp writes that a few of the "better floating houses were moored near gambling barges off Jones Point or off Alexandria's ferry dock

or at Jackson Street (Virginia end of the 14th Street Bridge)." There were several smaller ark colonies, Tilp continued, in this "womanizing business near Aqueduct Bridge for the poor to fair Georgetown trade." Occupants, as it turned out, were free from real estate tax, municipal building codes, and health regulations. He states that five such houses keep their clientele happy around Mallows Bay. What Tom and I were seeing was a piece of history that we were sure the Mount Vernon Chapter of the Daughters of the American Revolution would rather see eliminated altogether.

Tom and I suddenly became aware that, while we were taking in much of what the river had to offer, we had traveled only a few miles down the river. Point Lookout and Smith Point Lighthouse were still many miles ahead of us. When John calculated the time to return from the Smith Point Lighthouse back to Occoquan, it was agreed to just point the boat downstream and take off.

Again we headed downstream, passing Douglas and Smith Points along the Maryland shore, and Aquila Creek on our right. Aquila lays claim to the first English-speaking Catholic colony in Virginia. Aquila also commemorates the arrival of Spanish missionaries who landed here in September 1570 and were massacred by the Indians five months later.

Our attention was drawn to waving arms aboard another boat. Throttling back to neutral, John allowed the forward motion of the Chris-Craft to coast up to the waving arms where we found three people needing assistance. They said they had motored out yesterday at sunset from Aquila Creek to do some fishing and beer drinking. The evidence was there: empty beer cans scattered about the boat and the fishing rods tucked away in a rack. They said they had noticed leaking oil as they headed out yesterday evening, but thought little of it until their engine seized up. Lacking any night distress signals except a flashlight, and having no radio to call for help, they simply dropped anchor and waited until dawn. By then they figured someone would see them waving their arms. They figured right. We towed them back into Aquila Creek, passing Brent Point and dropped them off at Thorney Point.

We soon moved back into the Potomac, past Marlboro Point, Potomac Creek and Fairview Beach on the Virginia side. Some people say that this is the Potomac Creek where Pocahontas saved Captain John Smith from her father Powhatan. If so, Pocahontas saved Captain Smith's scalp more than once, as these stories abound all over the area. As we continued down the river John swung his boat toward the Maryland shore so that we could get a better view of two large dish antennas at Maryland Point. Then it was back over to the Virginia side where we passed Somerset Beach and rounded Metomkin Point to our right. We were amazed at the erosion damage caused by the Potomac on the Virginia shoreline. The erosion was so bad we saw a corner of an old barn hanging over the edge of an embankment above the river. Swinging back toward the Maryland shoreline, we passed a boathouse near Riverside, Maryland, and, using binoculars, looked north up Nanjemoy Creek. Also to our north was Port Tobacco River flowing down into the Potomac

from Maryland. John abruptly turned the boat east and followed the Potomac around Mathias Point. Just a few hundred feet off Mathias Point, and still miles from the Chesapeake Bay, is the deepest point along the entire length of the Potomac. It is over 120 feet deep. The sheer volume of water undercutting a gorge as the river turns a sharp corner and heads eastward causes the extreme depth. As we turned eastward the Governor Harry W. Nice Bridge, also called the Route 301 Bridge or the Potomac River Bridge, came into view. The bridge is the longest spanning bridge to cross the Potomac and is one of only two toll bridges that span the Potomac. The view of the bridge reminded me of an earlier trip Tom and I had taken.

We had pushed the inflatable boat into the Potomac water from the Maryland shore in the shadow of the Route 301 toll bridge. Our goal had been to take photographs of the bridge for a painting. Where we almost had to duck to pass under the Potomac's first bridge near the Fairfax Stone, the Route 301 Potomac River high level fixed bridge had a vertical distance of 135 feet.

Our shallow draft inflatable with its small 5 horsepower Chrysler outboard motor was once the king of the shallow Potomac River above Great Falls. Now it had been reduced to serfdom by the monster inboard-outboard racing boats and boat hulls weighed down with oversized Yamaha, Mercury and Evinrude marine engines. The tranquility of the river was shattered on this weekend as hundreds of boat owners, abandoning their winter cocoons, stretched their wings and flew across the waters. Meanwhile, we listened and constantly watched out for boats coming near.

We motored upstream along the Maryland shore and came to a "bar and grill" built up over and into the Potomac. The sign above the building read 'Capt Billy's Crab House.' It was a hangout, from what we saw, for those who looked like they had recently turned legal drinking age. In this maritime community, though, the powerboat had replaced the hot rods. We came up near Billy's pier that was loaded with boats whose sterns were sitting much lower in the water than the rest of the hull. There were huge single and twin outboard motors sitting quietly but menacing. Moving back and forth in front of the pier like a shark was a Maryland Marine Police boat. The uniformed officer behind the wheel weaved his boat around and inspected the other boats and the people heading in and out from the pier. We saw some teenagers in one boat pouring their cans of beer into the Potomac from the stern of their boat when the police boat turned away for a moment.

We looked around at the other piers sticking out into the Potomac and found one lone sailboat. It was nestled up alone against the very end of the pier, looking castigated by the powerboats waiting to leap across the waves at the turn of a key and a push of a button.

We felt out of place there, two guys in an inflatable boat with a small engine and taking pictures, so we motored on and turned to head back toward the bridge and the camper. After lunch, we headed downstream to Cobb Island.

We first passed beneath the Blue Star Memorial Highway that crosses the Route 301 Bridge and then we passed a power plant on the Maryland shore much like the PEPCO power plant near Quantico. Rounding a small spit of land called Lower Cedar Point, we continued past Morgantown and headed downstream toward Cobb Island. Morgantown is a place well-known for its excellent fishing and oystering since it was founded in the 1700s. A ferry used to operate from here to Potomac Beach in Virginia before the Potomac River Bridge was built two miles behind us. Our small engine was full open but far underpowered compared to the other boats zooming by in deeper waters. We passed tilled farmland that looked no different from what you would see in Kansas. These farmlands, though, butted up against a shoreline and you could see, mixed in with the more typical farm equipment like tractors and combines, old boats sitting tilted on the ground or on rusting boat trailers and marine engines sitting on blocks. Remnants of old piers could be seen sticking out like fingers extending out into the Potomac, waiting to grab little boats that wandered too close to shore. After passing many hidden coves and nooks, we reached Swan Point, giving up on the slow but wet trip to Cobb Island and returned to the Route 301 Bridge.

Back to today's final trip down the Potomac, we again passed under the Route 301 Bridge and were amazed at how fast the Potomac doubled, if not tripled, in width. The last time we did this, we were in an inflatable. Tom and I hugged the Maryland shoreline and never really thought about the Virginia side of the Potomac. This time, though, we had intersected the bridge in the middle of the river and both shores fell away from our view. It was now going to be harder to swing back and forth from shore to shore on our downstream journey. Having seen the Maryland shore down to Swan Point on the previous trip, we decided to head for another familiar sight on the Virginia side, Colonial Beach, once called the "Las Vegas on the Potomac."

There was no doubt that from the Route 301 Bridge the Potomac widens considerably. From then on it continues to widen, influenced by the estuaries dumping into the river. The river continues to be mixed by the fresh and brackish waters from the estuaries and the salty waters from the Atlantic pushing up the Chesapeake and into the Potomac. As the silt-laden Potomac River widens it also becomes sluggish - no longer running downstream from higher elevations but being pushed along by the fresh Potomac waters behind it. From here the Potomac flows through flat tidewater country. The most important Maryland tributaries we saw as we motored downstream were the Port Tobacco River, the Wicomico River and St. Mary's River. These tributaries drain St. Mary's, Charles and Prince George's Counties and flow south or southwest. Below Allen's Fresh at Maryland's Route 234 it becomes the much wider Wicomico River.

We passed a lonely expanse of military barbed-wired fences and towers belonging to the Naval Surface Weapons Center in Dahlgren Bridge was uneventful compared to an earlier trip Tom and I had made.

We were again in our inflatable boat, but with a slightly more powerful engine. We put in at Stony Point on the Virginia shore just upstream from Colonial Beach.

This time we headed toward Colonial Beach, and thought we had reached the beach based on the noise coming from an area up ahead of us. We weaved our way around some cruising motorboats and found ourselves, instead, at Potomac Beach, where a live band was entertaining a small group of people at the baseball field. We rounded Bluff Point and stayed close to shore. When we arrived at Colonial Beach the traffic congestion on the water was as bad as the traffic we saw on shore. At one time Colonial Beach was the premier beach along the Potomac, with legalized gambling, a boardwalk and fairgrounds with rides. Those with metal detectors can still find fairground tokens buried in the sand.

We motored around the southern tip of Colonial Beach, entered Monroe Creek and came up to the Colonial Yacht Center marina. We killed the engine and drifted up to one boat where we talked to an elderly couple who were on their sailboat, sitting in the stern near the wheel. We went ashore to buy some refreshments from the marina's snack bar and when we returned they were still there. We thanked them for watching our boat, wished them good sailing and headed back into the Potomac.

For today's final ride, we were again off Colonial Beach and John was throttling back to avoid swamping some jet-skiers. When we looked behind us, we noticed that these jet-skiers were running full-bore at the wake that John's boat was making and slamming right into it. When the jet-skiers hit the wake they would be thrown a couple of feet into the air before hitting the water again. Some even lost their balance and fell off their jet-skis into the water. The jet-ski would automatically return to idle and begin turning in a small circle. The kid would swim back to it, climb back on to it from the rear, and hit the throttle again to go find another wake to jump.

Unimpressed with the congestion of boats, John headed down the Virginia shore, past Mattox Creek and Popes Creek. George Washington was born on his father's Popes Creek tobacco farm on February 22, 1732. He lived there until he was nearly 4 years old, and again for several years as a teenager. Today, a Memorial House stands near the site of the original house, which burned down in 1779. Ever since John Smith sailed up the river he was to call Potomac, the livelihood of most people along the Potomac consisted of working on farms and plantations. At the George Washington Birthplace site, operated by the National Park Service, interpreters in authentic garb cook on an open hearth, raise tobacco, corn and wheat, and generally make it seem as though you had traveled back in time 200 years to a colonial farm, complete with all the sights, sounds, and even smells of 18th Century plantation life—a life that influenced the character and development of the young Virginian who became the "Father of Our Country." Gazing out from our boat in the Potomac, I expected to see a four-masted sailing ship to come up the Potomac, loaded with cotton and heading for Alexandria. Just

downstream from George Washington's birthplace on the Virginia shore we passed by a huge brick house sitting on a bluff overlooking the Potomac. This was Stratford Hall, the birthplace of Robert E. Lee who became the General in Chief of the Confederate Armies. The crib he slept in is still at Stratford Hall. It was Thomas Lee, a prominent Virginia planter, who built Stratford in the late 1730s. Using brick made on the site and timber cut from the nearby forest, builders and craftsmen constructed the H-shaped house, coach house and stables. The Great Hall in the center of the house is 29 feet square. What was even more interesting to me than all this information was what Tom said to me. It seems his ancestry, according to stories his grandparents used to tell, goes back to this Lee family.

We passed over the remains of the Civil War ship TULIP. All that is left of the screw steamer TULIP, after one of her two boilers blew up, is some rotten wood that can still be dived on. I dived on TULIP years ago, but the current and visibility during the summer forced me to grab on to anything I could find and move very slowly. Research told me that the gunboat sank carrying a 20-pounder Parrott rifle, two 24-pounders, and two heavy 12-pounders. I never saw the cannon. It was the most I could do to hold on to the wooden remains against the current, but the story still goes that at least one cannon never was found and is still down there.

Never having had his boat beyond the Route 301 Bridge, John was beginning to feel comfortable with the wide expanse of water. Down in these parts of the

Potomac, the waves felt a little bigger as we continued toward our final rendezvous point.

It was then that John saw the cliffs along the Virginia shore: Horsehead, Stratford and Nomini Cliffs rising yellowish white almost straight up off the beach. He slowed to ask us what these cliffs were doing here in the Potomac.

The cliffs at Westmoreland State Park are called Horsehead Cliffs and they are similar to the more popular and advertised Calvert Cliffs along the Chesapeake Bay. Both cliffs contain the fossilized remains of manatees, sharks, porpoises, crocodiles and seashells - some as much as 15 million years ago. In these cliffs are a great many fossils, from tiny organisms to the remains of 35-foot ancestors of today's whales. You are not allowed to pry anything loose from the cliffs; you can take anything you find underwater or lying loose off the beach. For those who would rather view today's living creatures, over a hundred species of birds have been recorded within the confines of Westmoreland State Park.

John had checked the chart and said that we had missed Cobb Island. He asked us if we wanted to backtrack and head back over to the Maryland side.

There was no need. Tom and I had put the inflatable boat in the Potomac to check out Cobb Island months ago. That time, though, remembering the drenching we took on our Route 301 Bridge excursion, we drove to Cobb Island and simply used the boat to go around the island.

We launched from the crowded marina at Neale Sound, which separates Cobb Island from the main Maryland shoreline. We circled the island, watching everyone in their yards with barbecues smoking and lawn chairs filled to capacity. When we had gone half way around the island, pushed into the Potomac River by the waters of the Wicomico River, we saw an opening of beach that wasn't fenced. Ashore, we discovered that Cobb Island played a part in radio history. In December 1900, Reginald Aubrey Fessenden and Frank W. Very were experimenting in wireless telephony. For the first time in radio history they succeeded in sending and receiving intelligible speech by electromagnetic waves. This was accomplished between two masts 50 feet high and one mile apart.

We shoved off from Cobb Island and completed the self-guided tour. Two months earlier we had been standing in the snow in the center of the Potomac River at the Fairfax Stone and getting only the soles of our shoes wet. We even straddled the river at the Fairfax Stone, one foot in Maryland and one in West Virginia. Now, at sea level, the river was 60 feet deep in places and 3 miles wide.

We didn't return to Cobb Island, but we reminded John not to forget St. Clement's Island. It wasn't that we had not visited this island either during our wanderings. It was just that we wanted to show John that 40-foot white cross sticking up from the island. We had been there before, October 8th to be exact.

On that day, Tom and I drove down to Colton's Point, Maryland, to attend the 22nd Annual "Blessing of the Fleet" sponsored by the Seventh District Optimist Club. One of the main attractions for us was to get back out on the Potomac and boat over to St. Clement's Island. This time it was on an oyster boat called FREE SPIRIT. Once on the island, Tom took an additional trip on the Potomac by riding the "water taxi" out from the island for some photography. Once on the island, we listened to live music; watched Belgian horses pulling 8,000-pound sleds of concrete blocks across the grass; watched Miss St. Mary's County do a hula dance in a grass skirt; inspected a wig-wam, a duck-blind, a Maryland State Police medical evacuation helicopter, a speedboat named Miss Budweiser; and we listened to a group of people dressed as Confederate soldiers talk about how the Union had not only won the Civil War but also won the rights to the history of the War, and how they were out to correct them. Like at all such gatherings, we ate, from the traditional crab cake sandwiches and crab soup to the less traditional Greek gyros. What was all this about and what did the Potomac have to do with it? Simply, it had everything to do with the Potomac and Maryland.

In March 1634 a group of English settlers boarded two boats, ARK and DOVE, crossed the Atlantic, and sailed into the Chesapeake Bay. They sailed for some 73 more miles until they reached the bay's second largest tributary - the Potomack. While sailing up the Potomac, they remembered tales told to them of the local Indians who were not too thrilled about having colonists claim the land as theirs on behalf of the colonist's government. Colonists, on the other hand, thought it was comical that these Indians believed that no one could actually own land. Still,

the colonists chose to land safely on an island instead of the mainland just in case. This happened to be St. Clement's Island, where the colonists proceeded to take possession of the land and call it Maryland, after their queen. One colonist was a Roman Catholic priest, Father Andrew White, who then celebrated the first Roman Catholic Mass in the English-speaking colonies on that island. So the two-day annual event is a celebration of what happened over 350 years ago. Thanks must go to the Seventh District Optimist Club for recognizing the importance of this event, and for saving the island. The 40-foot white cross rises from the island and can be seen from many miles away. At the base of the cross is a sign that reads:

"ST CLEMENT'S ISLAND

To this island in March 1634, Governor Leonard Calvert and the first Maryland colonists came in the vessels Ark and Dove. Here they took possession of the province of Maryland, erected a cross of Maryland wood, and celebrated the Holy Sacrifice. Here they first brought to the New World those principles of religious liberty which have been the chief glory of this State."

Two weeks after landing, the colonists, led by Leonard Calvert who was the brother of Lord Baltimore, went on to establish the first permanent Maryland settlement at a nearby Roman Catholic town called St. Mary's City. In 1669 St. Mary's City became the capitol of the colony until 1694 when it was moved to Protestant Annapolis. A reproduction of the original capitol building may now be seen at St. Mary's City. The colonists soon began trading with the Indians, exchanging trinkets and cheap liquor for furs and other items that sold well back in the Old World. A Mr. West purchased Tangier Island in the Chesapeake Bay from the Pocomoke Indians in 1666 at a cost of two overcoats. Eventually, the Indians figured out how to get even - they taught the colonists how to grow and smoke tobacco.

The "tobacco society" grew into large plantations, with wealthy landholders turning southern Maryland and parts of Virginia into a one-crop economy. By the 1650s, the Virginia and Maryland colonies were exporting almost five million pounds of tobacco a year. By 1700, tobacco made up four-fifths of the value of British North America's exports. Poor agricultural practices led to the decline of tobacco culture, with much land returning to forests.

St. Clement's Island today is only about one-third its original size. The rate of erosion was so severe during the 1960s that the island was about to disappear altogether, swept downstream by the persistent Potomac. The Seventh District Optimist Club stepped in, and chiefly through their efforts, the Maryland Legislature appropriated the funds necessary to preserve the "Birthplace of Maryland" for future generations. Now the club holds the annual "Blessing of the Fleet" from the island. What is a "Blessing of the Fleet?" It

Events on the Potomac — Blessing of the Fleet at St. Clements Island.

is when all the freshly-painted fishing boats would set sail for the new season, flying colorful pennants and honking their horns amid a frenzied celebration. With a priest in the lead boat sprinkling holy water on the waters ahead of them, the fishing fleet would sail around the harbor and out into the ocean. Their prayers would be for a fruitful season. These "Blessings of the Fleets" occur all over the world, including here on the Potomac.

As with anything or anyone you meet for the first time, you tend to first view them as strangers, and the Potomac is no exception.

You can drive over it by bridge every day but not really get to know it. It takes some familiarity with the river before you get to understand and appreciate it. One thing that struck me as having finally gotten to know the river was when Tom and I stepped off the boat onto St. Clements Island. There, nestled against the pier, was the tugboat "Cap't Tom," complete with barge. It was a year ago, almost to the day, when on a trip from Woodbridge to Georgetown we passed by "Cap't Tom" pushing a barge downstream from Washington. It was one of Tom's first watercolor painting for this book, and the painting was meant to illustrate that people still made a living plying the Potomac waters. Few commercial enterprises these days use the Potomac to make a living, although one can still see the occasional Steuart Petroleum barge and the small ocean-going freighters delivering newsprint to the Robinson Terminal Warehouse in Alexandria once a week. A few sand and gravel barges scurry about on the Potomac, but today, the tugboat company's Port Engineer invited us on board for a tour

of their commercial tug "Cap't Tom." Although this was our first time on the boat, it really felt familiar and made me feel like we had gained a sense of achievement with the river. It confirmed our initial perception that this tug belonged in this book. Tom, who had come to know the boat in detail through the hours spent painting it, had the same feeling of accomplishment. He felt that what we had set out to say and show in the book from the original brainstorming between ourselves was finally coming to fruition. The tugboat company, Florida Rock Industries, owns six such boats in the Potomac and Chesapeake area. The tugs are used mostly for moving rock and sand, but it was meeting "Cap't Tom" again at the "Blessing of the Fleet" that really struck us as appropriate.

Back on Colton's Point, we toured the St. Clement's Island and Potomac River Museum. The museum tells the story of the Island and the people who have lived along the banks of the Potomac. The library was very impressive, with its walls lined with old photographs of lighthouses that dotted the shores of the Potomac at one time or another. Our tour guide was a direct descendent of the owners of the Island. I could not imagine a happier person than this one as she presented the museum to us, pointed out the collection of Indian arrowheads and the antique baby carriages, talked about her family genealogy, and showed off the excellent paintings by George F. McWilliams. Outside the museum sat a boat named "Doris C."

The DORIS C. is a Potomac River Dory and was built in 1919 by John Long for Captain Henry Gibson.

It was named the DORIS C. for Doris Cheseldine. The vessel was used continuously by Captain Gibson from 1919 to 1975. It was originally a two-masted sailing vessel, but it had been converted to power. Captain Henry Gibson donated it to the St. Clement's Island and Potomac River Museum in 1975. This Potomac River Dory is a fine example of a boat that represents the long heritage of the river and the men who harvested the seafood resources from the mid 1600's until present time.

It was back to the present with Tom and John as we tied up to the now lonely pier and walked around the island. We were soon back in the middle of the Potomac. With St. Clements Bay and Breton Bay on our left and Nomini Bay on our right, we headed for Ragged Point, Virginia.

After passing Lower Machodoc Creek and rounding Ragged Point, I noticed John was tapping the glass on the fuel level indicator. He throttled back just slightly and announced it was time for the boat's first drink of the day. Studying the charts and the inlets along the Virginia shore, we decided to head into Yeocomico River. Looking over at the Maryland shore, we noticed some fuel tanks and a lighthouse at Piney Point and a large pier jutting out into the Potomac. A little further on, we again looked north at the Maryland shore and saw St. George Island and the mouth of St. Mary's River. Having reached Yeocomico River, John had to keep his boat well outside Lynch Point. When we had threaded our way around pound nets staked line-abreast into the waters from shore and rounded the channel marker, John tapped his

fuel gauge again and concluded that he could go a little further. We continued down Cherry Point Neck to Coan River. Here we discovered a refueling stop on a half-moon-shaped peninsula called Lewisetta, Virginia. It was a little past noon, and the place looked deserted. As we tied up alongside the refueling pier, a man came out of the general store (which was also the town's Post Office and general meeting place), wandered down the pier and took care of us.

We reboarded the boat and cast the lines off while the man who had stood at the pump pushed us away from the pier.

We were now running parallel with the Virginia shoreline, the Maryland shoreline lost in the haze. We passed Bay Quarter Neck, Neuman Neck, Hull Neck, Mob Neck, and Hack Neck. After passing several homes dotting the Virginia shoreline, we finally arrived at the southernmost portion of the mouth of the river, Smith Point. John Smith who also named a nearby island after himself during a 1608 trip up the Chesapeake Bay from Jamestown named this point. We could have turned into a narrow inlet and entered Little Wicomico River, but in the distance, through a light fog, was a faint red flash from Smith Point Lighthouse. That was our final destination and the end of our travels. One ship that uses this narrow passage often is CAPTAIN EVANS. Docked near Reedville, Virginia, which claims to be the center of the largest fishing industry in the United States, CAPTAIN EVANS will first slip from her dock and move down Sloop Creek and into Little Wicomico River. It then motors through the narrow channel and across 13 miles of Chesapeake Bay to Smith Island. Smith Island lacks a jail, police and elected officials. The island is also the last outpost of direct descendants of the original Bay Settlers from Cornwall, England, who arrived here in 1657. Religious dissenters from St. Clement's Island, with many dissenters converting from Roman Catholic to Methodist settled Smith Island. Even the Elizabethan accent lingers in their speech. While we strained our eyes through the binoculars to get a glimpse of Smith Island from Smith Point, we realized that another point of land much closer was also invisible in the mist: Point Lookout. This point, the northernmost portion of the mouth of the Potomac, was nowhere to be seen. Although it couldn't be seen this time, Tom and I will remember Point Lookout for some time.

Point Lookout was the site of a Civil War prisoner-of-war camp run by the Union. It was originally called Smith's Sparke Point, then renamed St. Mitchaell's Point by Leonard Calvert, Maryland's first Governor, and then Point Lookout. The word 'lookout' came about because in colonial times the settlers believed that by standing on the point one could see out to the Virginia Capes on clear days.

In our inflatable boat on a sunny summer day we came in on the Potomac side of Point Lookout and tried to find some respite from the increasing winds in a large open bight called Cornfield Harbor. It was still too exposed to the wind for our comfort, so we beached our boat and began walking along the western side of Point Lookout. It is a sandy beach and I had heard from Mike Freeman, owner of American Watersports in Oxon Hill,

Maryland, that thousands of seahorses come up here to spawn and raise their young in and around the reeds. That was enough on this hot day to convince us to don our SCUBA gear, grab the underwater cameras and see what was hiding in the reeds.

The wind had picked up considerably as we got back into our boat and approached the Chesapeake Bay. Looking back on Point Lookout, you could pick out the loblolly pines poised above the whitish sandy strips of the beach.

For some unexplainable reason, Point Lookout is a special place for migratory birds heading south for the winter. Birdwatchers are parked at Point Lookout mainly from fall through spring to watch the migration. They are not disappointed as whistling swans and Canada geese appear throughout this season. One winter at Point Lookout, as we continued our Potomac adventures, we sat in the car and watched ducks diving into the Potomac. It is worth the trip from Washington to smell the seawater in the air and watch these diving birds.

Other birds in this area include herons, egrets, Oldsquaws, all three species of scooter, red-breasted mergansers, both greater and lesser scaups, horned grebes by the hundreds, buffleheads, and canvasbacks. At the very end of Point Lookout, a series of wooden pilings juts out into the Potomac. Perched on these pilings were double-breasted cormorants and gulls. Cormorants are exciting to watch as they float on air currents above the waters, looking for small eddies in the water signifying fish close to the surface. Spying one, they tuck their wings in close to the bodies, and speed head first into the waters to grab dinner. The cormorants' feathers are not heavily oiled like other shore birds, and after a time they become waterlogged. So when you usually see them perched on the pilings with their wings outstretched, what they are doing is simply drying out their plumage before launching another strike.

Point Lookout is also the only known nesting area for the boat-tailed grackle on the western shore of Maryland. They usually are found on the eastern shore, across the Chesapeake Bay.

Tom and I had camped overnight a few weeks later at Point Lookout in preparation of watching and photographing the spreading sunrise coming over the eastern horizon. We were to be leisurely floating on the Potomac, cameras at the ready, to photograph a sunrise with Point Lookout in the foreground. I had faith Tom was going to turn this into a great watercolor painting.

Above us it was getting lighter. We could distinguish between the heavy clouds and the sky by the time we had inflated our boat and pushed off into protected Lake Conoy. This was our first try with a more powerful motor. The inflatable craft leapt up onto the water and planed toward the mouth of the lake and into Cornfield Harbor on the west side of Point Lookout. We passed by the Point Lookout boat ramp, but not without first noticing a white triangular flag whipping in the wind and trying to hang on to a National Park Service flagpole. The wind had changed direction since the previous night and was now coming out of the southeast. Tom and I wondered what we were about to get ourselves into; that white flag meant

small craft advisory with waves up to three feet. As we were leaving the protected bay we passed a small boat coming into the bay and Tom throttled back and passed close to the other boat's starboard. Two men surrounded with fishing gear were looking at us as we passed by, not waving, not saying a word, not even shaking their heads in disbelief. They looked tired. Our wives had gone back to sleep at the campgrounds and I began to wonder if going back to sleep wasn't such a bad idea after all.

The End of the Potomac — Smith Point Lighthouse

We left the lake and rounded Horseshoe Bend in Cornfield Harbor on the Potomac River. There was a little wave turbulence as the wind caught us. The first wave that met us broke over the bow and partially filled the boat and the bucket carrying the camera gear with water. To compensate for the breaking waves, Tom throttled the engine forward to get us up higher. That only made me fall backward off the front seat. I landed at Tom's feet, soaked and tasting the cold saltwater in my mouth. Forget sleep; the entire affair had shocked me awake.

I repositioned myself and hooked my legs beneath me, wrapping them around the seat while the waves continuing to toss us around like a toy. Once in better control of my balance, Tom gunned the engine and we were moving again. The camera gear was dried and stowed in the forward compartment. The bucket was used to bail water and we were soon back in some semblance of order. In less than 5 minutes we had gone from dry naive cock-sure sailors talking about the sun rising and camera F-stops to wet morose lubbers talking about drift directions if the engine was to conk out. We slowed again as I repositioned myself; I braced myself better and pulled back on the bowline to raise the bow slightly up and out of the water. Tom again throttled forward and we were soon bouncing around the waves. I felt like I was on a bronco at the rodeo. I wrapped the bowline around my left hand a few times while my right arm was held out for balance. Now it was Tom's turn to get wet. With the engine full out the salt spray created from hitting the crest of

a wave passed around me and hit Tom square in the chest. We were now heading for the whitecaps.

It had never occurred to us that trying to photograph in low light from a bouncing inflatable boat was just not going to work. When we finally arrived "on station," I pulled our camera gear out and Tom and I began setting up some shots. We had our lenses wide open and our light meters were telling us our exposures still had to be around 2 seconds. Being tossed about by the waves did wonders for our idea of a still picture. It appeared that we would have to stay on the water a bit longer and wait for the sky to lighten up a bit more.

It took less than 10 minutes for that to happen. The sun was already up and only hidden by the dark clouds. The clouds parted for awhile and we took some shots of Point Lookout, but not the picture-perfect images you see on postcards. Ours turned out gray and flat this time. The clouds reformed and pushed the sunlight away from our lenses. It began to rain, which didn't matter because we were soaked anyway. We bagged this trip and decided to return later; Tom turned the boat around and headed back to camp. On the way back we went out of our way to pass by two barges that had been anchored in the harbor. As we neared, we disturbed the hundreds of seagulls and a few cranes that had been sleeping. They all took off, making a loud noise. They flew away together, gaining altitude, then slowly came into the wind in unison. They commenced flying toward us and dropping altitude in what I believed was going to be a classic bombing run on us. I just knew it, we were about to top off this wonderful experience by being crapped on by hundreds of seagulls. At the last second they broke off and returned to the barges, it stopped raining, and we went back to camp to dry off and eat breakfast. We were two guys surrounded with camera gear just looking at each other as we entered the protective area of the lake, not saying a word, not even shaking our heads in disbelief. We were tired.

Today was different. We were wide awake, had just finished eating the lunches we had brought with us, and were heading toward the lighthouse. Like a few weeks back, Tom and I noticed that the choppiness of the water had increased—the result of wind, tides, and two massive amounts of river water converging to become the Chesapeake Bay. At Harpers Ferry, we watched as the Shenandoah River lost its name when it merged with the Potomac; now we were witnessing the loss of the Potomac. The Potomac contributes about 18 percent of the total freshwater inflow to the Chesapeake Bay. We circled the lighthouse a few times, marveling at the decibel level of the foghorn as it tickled the hairs on the back of our necks when we were directly in front of it. We hardly heard it from the other side of the lighthouse. The red flashing light was now white. It was white when you were in the Chesapeake looking at it and red if you were between the lighthouse and the Virginia shore looking at it. A lone sailboat, sails stowed, decks clean and engine running, came out of the mist and passed between us and the lighthouse, heading north and directly into the wind. The two-person crew appeared to have returned from a long cruise; they looked tired and,

apparently concentrating hard on what lay ahead, and didn't return our wave. John had cut back his engine as we watched the sailboat move past, and now the sailboat slowly slipped back into the mist. Their journey was nearing completion; ours was now done.

When we returned to places we had previously visited along the Potomac, like the Paw Paw Tunnel on the C&O Canal, Harpers Ferry, Point Lookout, or Great Falls, we would never see them exactly the way we saw them the very first time. Floods had since toppled trees, friendships had strengthened, seasons and even the time of day had changed the look and feel of the river. This is the wandering of the Potomac. As much as the Potomac would change through the seasons, it was the Potomac that was here first, and it would always remain the same Potomac that Captain John Smith, President George Washington, Supreme Court Justice William Douglas, General Robert E. Lee, Tom and I, and many others, have come to experience and enjoy.

The downstream journey had ended.

About the Paintings

"I hope that some of the readers of this book purchased or received this book because they also admire the work of watercolor artists or are artists themselves. During past art shows of my work, the one question most often asked is about my technique – "How do you capture such fine detail with watercolor?" Well, to answer that question, I must relate a story or two behind each painting in this book and the techniques used to capture my feelings that went into each painting. My comments are mostly off-the-cuff, jotted down while I painted, and left to Doug to edit. My desire is to produce a feeling of déjà vu - that is, having seen my paintings in this book and then later, upon traveling and visiting the site of one of these paintings for the first time, I hope you will get a feeling that you had been there before.

"My basic technique for capturing a scene in watercolor is to shoot the scene with my camera. For this book, over 1,200 positives (slides) were shot. If a particular scene worked well as captured on film, it went directly to watercolor. The sailboat on the Potomac in front of the power plant is a good example of that. Often, though, my paintings were composite paintings - that is, I picked bits and pieces out of various slides and placed them into my painting. Now before you get upset, I only painted composite scenes when they could have existed in the first place. For example, a cold winter sky with high wispy clouds would never appear in a summer scene. In the painting of George Washington's Mount Vernon as seen from the Potomac, I removed the ugly green mobile home that was along the bank of the river. I never physically moved a building, or put a boat in a scene where, for example, someone would know that this vessel has a 20 foot draft and was sitting alongside a pier in 4 feet of water. Anyway, while I hope you enjoyed reading the book, I also hope you enjoyed the paintings. These informal comments, written in geographical order from the Fairfax Stone to the mouth of the river, should make the paintings that much more enjoyable."

—Thomas B. Sherman

CHAPTER ONE: From the Fairfax Stone, West Virginia to Paw Paw, West Virginia

1. ***Birthplace of the Potomac — The Fairfax Stone.*** In the spring of 1989, I traveled with Doug as far as we could upstream. He was insistent that this had to be done, that a book about a river should include its source. What we saw, having driven for hours along the back roads of West Virginia and Maryland, was at first somewhat disappointing - this small stream gurgling out of the side of a mountain was like any other stream gurgling out of the side of any other mountain. I could have taken a photo of another stream closer to home and called it the source of the Potomac. Having driven for hours and hiked up the side of the mountain in search of the source, I began getting a feeling about the Fairfax Stone that made it special. I'm not sure if it was the snow, the stone itself, the words on the plaque, or the long car ride and hike with a good friend that made this special, but I now can put a feeling with the painting. The trick, I was told by Doug, was to make the readers see this as THE beginning of the Potomac, a tall request.

To make the painting as special as the trip itself took two paintings. There is the more traditional painting of the Fairfax Stone that includes the replica of the original stone and the nearby commemorative plaque, all surrounded by the snow that had fallen that day. You cannot mistake this scene as it is not duplicated anywhere else. The second painting invokes the feelings and memories that I have of our trip. This painting shows the actual stream that comes bubbling out of the mountain and becomes the North Branch of the Potomac River, complete with icicles clinging to the overhanging rocks and the previous autumn's leaves still red and gold under the water. The painting of the stream and rocks best reflected our experiences along the river. Sometimes the details in this painting can draw you into the painting to analyze specific items, like the leaves under the water or the blades of grass sticking out of the snow. Other times you want to back away from the detail to appreciate the beauty of the entire painting. The same thing happened in our travels along the Potomac. Some areas of the Potomac, like Paw Paw, Harpers Ferry and Great Falls, we spent many hours researching and photographing. With other areas we had to step back and look at the entire stretch of the river to appreciate its beauty.

2. *The Fairfax Stone — a Close-up.* Finding it hard to put everything from the Fairfax Stone into one painting without losing something in the translation, I chose to do two paintings of the Fairfax Stone area. One was to concentrate on the very essence of Potomac waters as it trickled out of the mountain to form a small stream - the very birthplace of the Potomac River. The other one was to take a closer look at Fairfax Stone itself. I believe these first two paintings did exactly that.

CHAPTER TWO: From Paw Paw, West Virginia, to Harpers Ferry, West Virginia

3. *The Potomac Waters Sidetracked — Paw Paw Tunnel and the C&O Canal.* I think the Chesapeake and Ohio Canal - the C&O Canal - is one of America's greatest man-made projects. Along its 185 mile length that starts in Cumberland, I found the most intriguing portion of the canal to be along the Potomac and near the small town of Paw Paw, West Virginia. The canal, by the way, is filled with water from the Potomac River. The Paw Paw Tunnel allowed the sidetracked Potomac waters to take a shortcut through a mountain that reduced the 6 or 7 miles of winding river through Paw Paw Bends into a 3/5ths-mile length of water moving straight through a mountain, meeting up with the Potomac on the other side. It was a hot summer day when we visited the tunnel, yet the tunnel was as cool as any cave. The echo of water dripping from the roof into the canal was eerie, as were the bats hanging upside down from the bricks when we visited the tunnel again in the winter. As we completed the tour by walking out of the darkness of the tunnel into the sunlight, a picture formed in my head as I stared at the opening. The camera came out, I walked knee-deep into the water and shot the opening of the tunnel.

CHAPTER THREE: From Harpers Ferry, West Virginia, to Great Falls and the American Legion Bridge

4. *Playing on the Potomac — Tubing and Canoeing.* These scenes were captured while standing in the Potomac on the Maryland shoreline at Harpers Ferry, West Virginia, in the hot summer of 1988. One pleasure of this area is to rent inner tubes and float down the Shenandoah River. At Harpers Ferry, the Potomac and Shenandoah rivers merge - the painting is a couple in a rented canoe and a tuber both on the Potomac. The canoeing couple had come drifting from upstream Potomac, the tuber had come floating down from the Shenandoah; they, like the rivers, had merged at this spot. This showed much more pictorially what couldn't be seen showing these two great rivers merging.

5. *Crossing the Potomac — General Jubal Early Car and Passenger Ferryboat.* Not only is this the last surviving ferry boat that crosses the Potomac River, but it is a rare production of a ferry boat in that it is connected to the shores by a very strong cable. The cable stretches across the river and the gears and pulleys on the side of the ferry just pulls the ferry along the cable to either shore. Once we watched in utter fascination as a powerboat came screaming downstream and passed right over the cable with no difficulty. Good timing, as Doug and I were about to do the same with our inflatable boat. We visited the ferry more than once and got to talk to the man who ran the ferry. I'm sure he has answered the same questions hundreds of times, but he sure was interesting to talk to. While Doug crossed the river and talked with the ferryboat captain, I stayed on the shore and took pictures of the event. On the next crossing we all met each other and exchanged impressions on what this meant to the book. In painting this scene, I had some shots of the ferry taken from the middle of the river showing the ferry in the center of its crossing, but those shots were just too flat. In this instance, I took the liberty of gaining a little altitude by crawling up the side of the hill and shooting the ferry at an angle that included, more appropriately, both shorelines.

6. *The Power of the Potomac — Great Falls.* The most visited area Doug and I photographed was Great Falls, both from the Maryland and Virginia shorelines. Every conceivable angle was shot in all seasons and one wintry scene I captured on film during the winter of 1989 reflected best what Doug was writing about when he used Great Falls as his 'sounding board' for his creation section of the chapter. We had literally hundreds of slides from Great Falls, views of rock climbers, kayakers, fishermen, views of the river at different flood stages after thunderstorms, trees with fall foliage or springtime buds, etc. Honestly, we have enough for a picture album just on Great Falls. Doug wrote a lot about how the Potomac was created in the Great Falls portion of the book. I wanted to capture that feeling of creation millions of years ago - of being there on a cold harsh day, gloomy and overcast, with roaring water and barren rocks, of something surreal that smacked of creation.

7. *Exercising On the Potomac — Rock Climbers at Great Falls.* Doug and I spent many hours around the Great Falls area of the Potomac. When friends come into town to play tourist and to visit places like the Smithsonian's National Air and Space Museum or to take the elevator to the top of the Washington Monument, both Doug and I always make sure that they also travel outside the Beltway and talk a walk along the paths that parallel both sides of the Potomac along Great Falls. During one particular summer we were on the Virginia side walking downstream toward Matildaville when we stopped to watch some young rock climbers practicing their hobby along the shore. Against the muddy, rapidly flowing Potomac waters, many adventure-seekers find enjoyment in challenging the sheer rock cliffs formed by the river at Great Falls. From Great Falls past Mather Gorge, the vertical cliffs work well for rappelling down or climbing back. When Doug and I first talked about what would make a good painting depicting exercising on the Potomac, the only thing we could think of was the more typical Georgetown crewing teams or the kayakers in the rapids. When we saw these rock climbers it became obvious that you didn't have to be ON the Potomac to exercise; you also could be exercising on something created by the river. There was also another reason the rock climbers attracted my attention. I saw in them the very real event of achieving a goal with a little thrill and danger mixed in. I like that, as my philosophy of life is that it is essential having some goals - with a little thrill and danger mixed in!

CHAPTER FOUR: From the American Legion Bridge to the Woodrow Wilson Bridge

8. *History of the Potomac — Georgetown Sculler.* While researching the book, the artist's wife, Marilyn, was working at Georgetown University. Her daily commute involved a 30-minute drive around the beltway, then a 30-40 minute ride on the Metro (subway); and finally a walk across the Francis Scott Key Bridge, twice daily. I wanted to capture how the Potomac River had some impact on Georgetown University. While on the bridge, you would quite often see the Georgetown scullers and crew teams practicing. The painting shows a sculler heading downstream. One of my shots caught the oars tossing some water up and out of the river for several strokes, which I kept in the scene I painted.

9. *Entertainment Along the Potomac — Kennedy Center at Dusk with Watergate.* This painting came about after some risk to the artist. As described in detail by Doug, I tried different dusk and nighttime shots of the Kennedy Center all along the Virginia shoreline of the Potomac, using different film speeds and lenses, but nothing worked the way I wanted to capture the building with its lights reflecting in the river's water. What I needed was an angle that could only be found standing at the water's edge from Theodore Roosevelt Island. Unfortunately I also wanted a night shot, so the National Park Service ranger was more than a bit upset when I came sauntering back across the bridge from the island after dark. The park closed at sunset and the ranger had to keep the gate open until I showed up, which was a bit past sunset! I had gotten the shot I needed, and my profound thanks to the National Park Service who Doug and I more than once pestered in our travels!

10. *Memorials along the Potomac — Arlington Memorial Bridge and Lincoln Memorial.* Most of the major monuments and memorials could be seen from the Potomac as we drifted past the District of Columbia - the Washington Monument, Lincoln Memorial, Jefferson Memorial, and so on. One memorial though, the Lincoln Memorial, rests on the banks of the Potomac and is easily identifiable. Although the sculpture of Lincoln himself can only be seen from the other side, the monument has a tremendous power about it that evokes a certain mood in me. I had to shoot this scene several times to get the correct visual balance between the memorial, Memorial Bridge, and the Potomac. I tried different times of the day, and finally selected an hour before sunset on a hot summer day.

11. *Enjoying the Potomac — Tidal Basin Painting of the Washington Monument with Cherry Blossoms in Full Bloom.* This painting has a special meaning to me because it was painted for the cover of our book and it was also painted about the time my oldest son Patrick was born at Georgetown University Hospital. The Tidal Basin has a magical quality to it with the blooming cherry blossoms and daffodils. The area pictured is now near the home of the new Martin Luther King Jr. Memorial.

At first sight, I would say that the Tidal Basin has nothing to do with the Potomac River, and then upon reflection I realized that all that water had to come from somewhere, and that somewhere, of course, is the Potomac. Given that the canals were written about in length in this book because the water in the canals were actually the Potomac waters sidetracked, it was also appropriate to show the postcard-style painting of the Tidal Basin during cherry blossom season, a season in 1990 in which the blossoms opened up far earlier than expected.

We had taken many shots of the Tidal Basin but this one has always been my favorite. My favorite time of year to visit the Tidal Basin is probably the same as a million other people - when the cherry trees are in bloom. As I soon found out, though, painting cherry trees in bloom is very difficult. The cherry trees in bloom have a somewhat enigmatic quality about them; a quality mysterious and hard to explain - like, I guess, the mysterious Orient itself. At times the blooms appear white and other times a very pale pink; all depending on how long they have been in bloom, the time of day, and the amount of sunlight hitting them. The colors are most elusive in the soft morning haze. At sunset, the warm golden color of the setting sun can turn the blooms a soft peachy color. No matter what color the blooms are, the mass of blooms converge and show reflected in the Potomac waters of the Tidal Basin.

12. *Sculpture on the Potomac — "The Awakening."* Sometimes a completely innocuous item that you have seen many times before suddenly jumps out and bites you. There was a time I would have said "No" to putting this poor drowning creature into a watercolor painting. Then Doug, a trivia buff, found out this creature was rising up out of the ground, not sinking into it. The sculpture is called "The Awakening" and it was commissioned upon cleaning up the polluted Potomac to commemorate the return of sport fishing to the Potomac. That was the bite, I saw the sculpture in a different way, and it was then I put it down in watercolor.

While painting a scene, I will sometimes get this feeling that the painting wants to take off and head in a direction that my earlier sketches had not intended. A painting will sometimes rise from the canvas in an entirely different manner than what I had envisioned. When this happens, when the scene takes on a life and personality all its own, I can only shrug my shoulders and say, "Oh well." This was true for "The Awakening." I returned to the site more than once, in different seasons and times of day and shot it at many different angles, even standing on the hood of my car! Problems such as foreshortening and the manner in which the camera lens will distort or enlarge the things closest to you had been bothering me. Yet, when it came down to transforming the shots into watercolor, the final image was nothing like what I had previously shot, yet it captured the spirit of the work very well. As noted earlier in this book, "The Awakening" was excavated and removed from Hains Point on February 20, 2008, and then was installed at National Harbor located in Maryland just south of the Woodrow Wilson Bridge.

13. *Power on the Potomac.* While this scene may not be recognizable as a landmark, even to those who spend much time on the Potomac, it was still a scene that intrigued me. The contrast is immediately understood - the power plant produces power to keep the community moving (for a price), while the power of the wind keeps the sailboater moving down the Potomac (for free).

14. *The Polluted Potomac — Tire Beach.* In writing about the Potomac, Doug was not ready to let people forget the pollution that made the Potomac a cesspool for a time. The words I read demanded a strong image, but the pollution was gone - or so I thought until we motored up to this place unsuspectingly in our boat. Later, we stopped along I-295 just north of the Woodrow Wilson Bridge to get another perspective of the littered beach. We climbed down the side of the Interstate and were surrounded by all sorts of trash. Some you could tell were there temporarily - thrown down the banks until the next high tide or flood washed them further downstream. Some trash had been there for awhile and was slowly being covered by sand. The thing that struck me were the number of tires populating the beach. Some were resting on top of the sand and others were in various stages of being covered by the sand. I'm sure there were many already covered. We called this

Tire Beach. Some trash was natural - driftwood and tree trunks pushed ashore by the current, but most of the trash was the same you would see at a trash dump. Now that we had evidence of continuing pollution, it seemed we had an obligation to the Potomac to publicize it, so Doug wrote and I painted.

CHAPTER FIVE: From the Woodrow Wilson Bridge to the Chesapeake River

15. *Making a Living on the Potomac.* While in a Chris-Craft off Occoquan Bay heading up the Potomac toward Washington, D.C., this tugboat was captured on film pushing a barge loaded with sand downstream toward Occoquan, to be deposited near the Richmond, Fredericksburg and Potomac railroad bridge crossing the bay at Woodbridge in the fall of 1988. The sand is used to make concrete at a plant at the base of the bridge. I wanted to depict a scene that showed that there were people who still made their living plying the Potomac waters. It wasn't enough to show a boat pulling up crabpots or a deep-draft vessel steaming up the Chesapeake as viewed from the mouth of the Potomac. I wanted to capture a purely Potomac scene in which a living was being made as far upstream as I could. We would meet "Cap't Tom" repeatedly in our travels, and nothing seemed nicer than the unofficial tour we received on her during the Blessing of the Fleet at St. Clement's Island.

16 and 17. *The Historic Potomac — Mount Vernon and the Boathouse.* As with any scene, there comes a time when the post cards succeed in capturing just the right angle, scene, color of sky. Still, I had to see for myself and we took the boat out into the Potomac to see what Mount Vernon looks like from the river. The Mount Vernon gazebo/boat dock was too far away to get into the same painting, so it was painted separately. There was an awful green mobile home sitting on the shore that was painted out of the scene, but the post cards were pretty much right. When a scene works, it works. The boat dock was incorporated into the book as this was a part of Mount Vernon seen from the Potomac and rarely seen by visitors arriving by car or bus.

18. *Bridges across the Potomac — The Route 301 Bridge.* One thing that fascinated me was the variations of bridges that have been built in order for man, car, and trains to cross the Potomac. Some are simply culverts, some are toll bridges, some hand-made using little more than ropes and wooden boards that you must balance yourself on as you cross, some built with steel and concrete. Many washed downstream in floods, with only their stanchions left in silent testimony of a day long gone. The first bridge along the Potomac was little more than a few hundred yards from the Fairfax Stone and simply allowed cars on an unmarked dirt road heading into Kempton, Maryland, to drive over the tumbling stream. The last one was the Route 301 Bridge, seen here crossing the Potomac and framing a Maryland-based Potomac Electric Power Plant (PEPCO) power plant. In our weekend travels to different sections of the river, we passed over and under the Route 301 Bridge several times, but it was the early morning scenes that I enjoyed the most. In this case, it was the silhouette of the bridge against the early morning sky that most inspired me to paint this scene.

19. *Events on the Potomac — Blessing of the Fleet at St. Clements Island.* Sometimes a scene remains the same 364 days out of the year. Then that one day a year when something happens it should be captured on film. One such event is the St. Clements Island Blessing of the Fleet. The event, sponsored by the local Optimists Club, has been going on for some 22 years now, and it commemorates the first landing and first Roman Catholic Mass held on what is now the state of Maryland. A Blessing of the Fleet is a people's request to God to make this year a safe, fruitful and prosperous one for those who play and make their living on the water. We had visited the island before, but this time it was full of people eating, singing, and dancing.

Sometimes a scene screams out at you for attention and a 40-foot white cross sitting on Blakiston Island (St. Clements Island) in the Potomac does that for you. The Potomac is full of islands, some with strange names, some overcrowded with people who wanted to get away from it all, one a National Park, some disappearing with every flood, some even called islands but not really islands at all. Some were connected to the "mainland" by bridges, some were only accessible by boat, some were even off-limits even by boat with rude "No Trespassing" signs warning you to stay away. My favorite was the scene of Blakiston Island seen from our boat going up the western entrance of St. Clements Bay.

In this painting I tried to capture both the idea of the festive event with the image of the 40-foot white cross. While the event lasts a weekend, the cross is there year-round, and it is, therefore, this 40-foot cross with its reflection in the Potomac River that is the most dominant visual element in the painting.

20. ***The End of the Potomac — Smith Point Lighthouse.*** With 11 miles of water across the Potomac at its mouth, the slip of land I was looking at across the river from Point Lookout was Virginia. As we roared across the Potomac toward Virginia in a high-speed boat, it was only fitting that the end of the Potomac from the Virginia side also be commemorated, and the most apt place to do so was at Smith Point lighthouse. There are times when you cannot see the Virginia shoreline from Point Lookout, and you can never see the lighthouse. So we had to return to Virginia one last time to capture the end of the river. It was appropriate that we end in Virginia; the idea to do the book originated in Virginia; Doug and I both lived in Virginia when this entire process began. This idea of a beginning and an end fits the mood in this painting. When we visited the lighthouse, the trace of low clouds or fog had concealed the exact position of the sun and one could wonder if we were seeing a sunrise or sunset. In this final painting, the idea of sunrise or sunset is moot, as is the idea of beginning and end. For Doug and myself, it was the end of a three-year journey but only the beginning of understanding the Potomac River itself.

Index

About the Author

Douglas E. Campbell, Ph.D., was born on May 9, 1954, in Portsmouth, VA, and grew up as a Navy Brat, traveling all over the world and living next to U.S. submarine bases at such places as Holy Loch, Scotland; Rota, Spain; Pearl Harbor, Hawaii; and Charleston, South Carolina. The oldest of six children, he graduated from Kenitra American High School, Kenitra, Morocco, in 1972 – his 13th school. He received his Bachelor of Science degree in Journalism from the University of Kansas on May 24, 1976; the following day was commissioned at his Naval Reserve Officer Training Corps (NROTC) Unit as an Ensign in the United States Navy. He joined the U.S. Naval Reserve Program as an Intelligence Officer in 1980 and was transferred to the Retired Reserves as a Lieutenant Commander on June 1, 1999.

Dr. Campbell received his Master of Science degree from the University of Southern California in Computer Systems Management in 1986 and his Doctor of Philosophy degree in Security Administration from Southwest University in New Orleans, Louisiana, in 1993. Dr. Campbell is president and CEO of Syneca Research Group, Inc., a veteran-owned small business incorporated in 1995 supporting several Government and commercial clients. He currently resides with his wife Trish in Southern Pines, North Carolina.

Dr. Campbell recently completed a 3-volume set of books on U.S. Navy, U.S. Marine Corps and U.S. Coast Guard aircraft lost during World War II outside the Contiguous United States (CONUS). His 600-page book investigating the loss of the U.S. submarine USS DORADO (SS-248) during World War II as a result of "friendly fire" has received critical acclaim (www.ussdorado.com). For a complete list and abstracts of all his books go to www.syneca.com

Dr. Campbell's published works include:

Compu-terror: Computer Terrorism and Recovery from Disaster
ASIN B00071D2XO
Building a Global Information Assurance Program
(co-author Raymond J. Curts, Ph.D.)
ISBN 0-8493-1368-6
Volume I: U.S. Navy, U.S. Marine Corps and U.S. Coast Guard Aircraft Lost During World War II –
Listed by Ship Attached
ISBN 978-1-257-82232-4; eBook ISBN 978-1-105-16346-3
Volume II: U.S. Navy, U.S. Marine Corps and U.S. Coast Guard Aircraft Lost During World War II –
Listed by Squadron
ISBN 978-1-257-88139-0; eBook ISBN 978-1-105-19671-3
Volume III: U.S. Navy, U.S. Marine Corps and U.S. Coast Guard Aircraft Lost During World War II –
Listed by Aircraft Type
ISBN 978-1-257-90689-5; eBook ISBN 978-1-105-20089-2
USS DORADO (SS-248): On Eternal Patrol
ISBN 978-1-257-95155-0
Computer Terrorism
ISBN 978-1-105-22289-4
BuNos! Disposition of World War II USN, USMC and USCG Aircraft Listed by Bureau Number
ISBN 978-1-105-42071-9; eBook ISBN 978-1-105-53059-3
Patent Log: Innovative Patents That Advanced the United States Navy
(co-author Stephen J. Chant)
ISBN 978-1-105-62562-6
The History of North Carolina's Moore County Airport (SOP)
ISBN 978-1-300-98997-4
FLIGHT, CAMERA, ACTION! The History of U.S. Naval Aviation Photography and
Photo-Reconnaissance
ISBN 978-1-304-47173-4
U.S. Navy, U.S. Marine Corps and MATS Aircraft Lost During the Korean War
ISBN 978-1-304-61073-7; eBook ISBN 978-1-304-69633-5